ANOTHER CULTURE/ANOTHER WORLD

BY FATHER MICHAEL OLEKSA

ANOTHER CULTURE/ANOTHER WORLD

Cataloging-In-Publication Data

Oleksa, Michael, 1947-
    Another culture/another world / by Father Michael Oleksa.
    p. 160; 15.2 x 22.9 cm.
Published by: Association of Alaska School Boards.
    Includes bibliographical references.
ISBN: 1-57833-301-6

    1. Indians of North America – Alaska -- Social life and customs.
    2. Eskimos – Alaska -- Social life and customs. 3. Acculturation
    – Alaska. 4. Multiculturalism – Alaska. 5. Ethnology -- Alaska.
    6. Alaska – Social life and customs. I. Title. II. Association of
    Alaska School Boards.

    E78.A3O44 2005

ACKNOWLEDGEMENTS

Produced and edited by Peter Metcalfe
Copy editing by Liz Dodd
Graphic design by Sue Kraft
Project management by Steve Nelson,
    Public Information Coordinator, AASB/Alaska ICE
Project initiated by Shelly Eidsness, AASB.

Cover images by Peter Metcalfe; access to indigenous artifacts courtesy of
Steve Henrikson, the Alaska State Museum.

For my three grandsons:

Joshua, Anthony, and John Michael (Jack)

and in memory of

Anna (Dorosz) Oleksa,

Michael and Doris M. (Conrad) Oleksa,

Adam and Nastasia (Daweak) Andrew,

Annabelle (Iguaq) Olick and Sven D. Haakanson, Sr.,

whose stories have enriched

and will always be part of my own.

CONTENTS

FOREWORD

As a mosaic of many cultures, Alaska enjoys a strength born of understanding and sharing the positive assets of our diverse communities. So, in our role as advocates for youth and education, the Association of Alaska School Boards (AASB) is pleased to present *Another Culture/Another World* by Father Michael Oleksa.

Education does not happen in the classroom alone—it is an ongoing process that involves teachers, parents, community members, elders and other adults who play a significant role in a young person's life. Recognizing this need, AASB launched the Alaska Initiative for Community Engagement (Alaska ICE) to move Alaskan communities towards greater student success by building strong youth-adult relationships.

The best chance we have to raise healthy, successful young people is when we all work together to provide the greatest opportunities for them to succeed, not only in school but also in life. Understanding one another's cultures, values and perspectives is an important part of building communities that support young people, and it is our hope that this book is a positive step towards that goal.

While Alaska is a young state, it is a land of ancient traditions. Father Michael reminds us that in a time not so long ago, Aleuts sailed into the world to become explorers and cartographers, and even before the social and political struggles of the 1960s, Tlingits fought for and won civil rights. These are stories worth learning and passing on to the next generation.

Through legends such as *The Eye of the Needle* and *Salmon Girl*, the author illustrates what subsistence means to the sociology, anthropology and spiritual life of Alaska's indigenous cultures. The brief essays that follow each legend help bring clarity to an often-misunderstood way of life.

The many languages of Alaska are also explored in this book. Father Michael explains how a root Yup'ik word, properly fitted with prefixes and suffixes, can convey as much information as an English sentence. Yet, as a bilingual speaker sharing his background with Yup'ik high school students, the author also shows us in a light-hearted way that words often are understood correctly only within their cultural context.

Publication of *Another Culture/Another World* coincides with development of an Alaska history curriculum for high school students. It is AASB's hope that books such as this can serve as an important supplement to the larger discussion of Alaska cultures and histories. We encourage educators, students, and parents—anyone with an interest in a life-enriching experience—to read this book. May *Another Culture/Another World* open the eyes and hearts of all who read it to the lessons and values that other cultures offer.

Carl Rose, Executive Director
Association of Alaska School Boards

INTRODUCTION

How do you respond when asked, What is your culture? How do you define or think of someone else's "culture"? Does everyone have one? Do you? Often when asked to describe our culture, we Americans first think of our ethnic background. "I'm part English, part Scottish, part French and a little German." Tribal peoples usually list their official tribal status as their culture. Immigrants may name their ancestral homeland. Or some of us may claim multiple backgrounds, saying "I'm a mutt." Or "I'm Heinz 57!"

But none of these represents the best description of culture. Although the term defies a hard and fast definition, a good way to think of culture is "the way we see our world." Because culture is more a view than a thing, it is invisible to us. Like a car's headlight, our cultural view does not shine back on itself, but illuminates what is in front of it. While we may apply cultural constructs to make sense of reality, they are invisible to us while we are using them—which is nearly all the time.

Several years ago, a friend of mine, Elaine Griffin of Chiniak, Alaska, shared an essay with me titled "Meditation in a Tool Shed," written by the British academician and lay theologian, C. S. Lewis. In this essay, the author imagines entering a dilapidated tool shed on a sunny day, where the old, warped-boarded roof and walls allow plenty of sunlight to stream through. When first entering, the beams of sunlight appear as bars of brightness dissecting the interior darkness of the shed. He can see each particle of dust as it dances around in a bar of sunlight. Then he moves his head a short distance and looks out, along the sunbeam, through the cracks in the roof, to the leafy tree branches outside, and beyond to the blue sky, white clouds and the sun itself, 94 million miles away. As he does this, the tool shed disappears, and any sense that this beam of light looked like a narrow golden ray also is lost. Looking *at* the sunlight is one experience, looking *along* it is totally different. And you cannot do both at the same time.

We look along our own culture, into the world beyond, but because it is the very means by which we see everything else, we cannot look at it simultaneously. Looking at our own culture, even partially, becomes possible only when we leave it. When we travel abroad we begin to recognize how much our own culture affects the way we understand and see the world. When visiting Europe, for example, most Americans immediately recognize how "American" they are, just as when in America, Europeans can see how "European" they are. This ability to recognize your cultural attributes when removed from your culture—that is, when you are forced into the role of "outsider"—reveals a cultural dynamic familiar to any minority population. As perpetual outsiders, minorities in any society are forced by the surrounding majority to look at as well as along their culture every day.

Each culture constitutes another universe, or another way of seeing reality. Through the people we meet over the course of our lifetimes we are all offered opportunities to enter into and explore other worlds—if we can learn to venture with curiosity into the stories of our friends and neighbors. If the stories told in our own communities take us to nearby planets, the stories in this book offer the possibility of visiting more distant galaxies.

The absorption of a community's stories into the thoughts and behaviors of its young people is also what we call "culture." This definition lends more objectivity to the idea of culture than does "the way we see the world." If we remember our family's stories and reflect upon how these have influenced our values and our behaviors, we can begin to look into what we could before only look along. We can also begin to listen to and appreciate the stories of other cultures, gaining insight into the way others see the world—the game of life as they play it.

Because other peoples' stories can at first be perplexing, or sometimes seem simplistic or obscure at first glance, each of the following chapters devoted to an indigenous culture of Alaska opens with a description of its storytellers' world view—the game of life and the rules by which the story's culture plays, and out of which the story emerged. Most of these stories have been passed along from generation to generation, over a span of centuries. On the one hand, each story is filled with wisdom and insight unique to its specific culture; on the other hand, all tap into universal aspects of human experience.

The introductions and notes to each story are intended to provide a way of understanding the story's meaning as it was known to those who originally told and heard it. The introductions aspire to provide enough background and context so that the reader can enter this other universe and see the images and characters, as well as the action of the story, from the perspective of its original narrators.

This book is an invitation to enter the stories of others, at the core of each may be discovered the secrets of our common humanity. It is an invitation to look along the beams of sunlight that penetrate this shared "shed" of our experiences as Alaskans, and that beckon us out into a wider and more vivid world.

In cultures with strong oral traditions, it is not uncommon for such stories to acquire the esteem one might expect of clan or family heirlooms—treasures not to be trifled with by outsiders. The traditional stories in this book are presented having fully observed the respective cultural protocols.

I hope you will enjoy these stories—not just as entertainment, but as prisms through which we may come to know and appreciate each other in all our complexity and beauty.

Michael J. Oleksa
Atertayagaq Ku̲xwoosgáax̲.
February 1, 2005

[Please turn to page 153 for a map illustrating the ethnographic regions of Alaska.]

Preceding page: Fourth of July at Black River fishcamp. *Photo by James Barker*

Athabascan children at the edge of a river. *Photo by Bill Hess*

Basketball game in Angoon. *Photo by Peter Metcalfe*

DIFFERENT SETS OF RULES

Culture is "the game of life as you understand and play it." Each cultural group plays the game of life differently, just as players in different sports use different skills and equipment, applying different rules to score points and win games.

Some games, for example, are timed. Basketball, football, hockey—and certainly all races—are won by the clock. Whoever has the most points when the time expires, or whoever crosses the finish line first, wins. Other games are not timed at all. Baseball, tennis, golf, poker, chess and billiards rarely rely on clocks and often ignore them completely. The game has an internal structure of its own which determines how long it will be played. Cultures are like this too. Some rely heavily on calendars, schedules and appointments, while others tend to operate along very different principles.

Clocks are an urban invention. The idea of dividing the day into twenty-four hours with sixty minutes to each hour and sixty seconds to each minute first arose in ancient Mesopotamia, modern day Iraq, within the first urban centers. City folks needed to keep appointments, arrange meetings, and stay "on time." Unable to see everyone in town at a glance, as could residents in the small villages, and not wanting to "waste time," city folks needed some sort of common time management. So many of our expressions about time arise from the "game of life" as played in cities. To be ahead, on, or behind time; to save, lose or gain time; to manage, kill or serve time—all make sense to anyone who plays the urban game of life.

The ancient Greeks called this sort of time "Chronos" and we still call the time that is measured with clocks and calendars— the imaginary time that passes inescapably with each successive moment—"chronological" time. It is one of the distinguishing characteristics of the modern world that everyone on the planet now shares a common notion of this sort of time, so that in any airport (one prominent architectural expression of our new planetary culture) every passenger knows when to board the airplane "on time."

Some cultures play a "game of life" in which "being on time" is taken literally. Punctuality is a virtue to be cultivated in the young and demanded of the old. When a person is invited to dinner in such a society at six o'clock, for example, the host expects and the guest understands exactly what this means. The guest should arrive at precisely six that evening. The little hand on the six. The big on the twelve. And, ideally, the second hand is also sweeping across the upper arc of the face of the watch at the moment the guest arrives. This is a matter of understanding and appreciating one of the basic social skills in such a culture's game of life.

I grew up in a predominantly German immigrant neighborhood in eastern Pennsylvania where everyone on my mother's side of the family understood and played the game of life in this way. A host carefully strategized the timing of the meal, counting backward from the precise time the guests would sit at the table and the bread would come hot from the oven, to the time when the bread needed to begin baking. The entire meal was orchestrated with military precision so that each course would be ready exactly on schedule. The banquet would begin at 6:08 p.m. and end precisely at 9:46 p.m. local time. A late guest would throw all this careful planning off, displaying inconsideration if not absolute rudeness to his host, almost certainly never to receive another invitation. Lateness in this ball game was sinful and almost unpardonable, and it seemed such people were condemned to eternal damnation for being late.

Not all cultures operate this way. The Slavic relatives on my father's side were much more relaxed about time. Other than the timer on grandma's stove, timekeeping devices were absent from my Ukrainian Baba's home. Although my father's old neighborhood was less than a mile from our house, somewhere between the Irish and the Slovak neighborhood clubs that stood in between, we crossed over into a new cultural landscape. In my father's Slavic neighborhood, if someone said "Come over at 7 p.m.," no one understood this to mean "at exactly 7." Rather, both the host and the guests took this to mean "Come no earlier than 7. I won't be ready before 7, but anytime after will be fine." So guests would arrive at 7:10, 7:15, 7:35 and even 8:00. It really didn't matter because the first course would be finger food, cold appetizers, in Russian "zakuski," and some beverages. Once everyone had arrived, all would be invited to the table, but the host did not begin warming up the soup until all those invited had had a chance to relax and enjoy the first round of treats. Unlike the German meal, the Slavic feast might last until 10 p.m., but it could just as easily continue until 11:00, midnight or beyond. Some guests might still be there the morning of the next day!

After traveling in both Germany and Russia, I came to see how differently these two European cultures understood and played the ball game of life. It helped me understand my parents a lot better too! Every family excursion or trip began the same way. Mom had carefully calculated distance and driving time and established both an estimated time of arrival and an ENTD (estimated necessary time of departure) and gotten herself and the kids ready "in plenty of time." But we were always waiting for Dad, who as the ENTD approached, inevitably could still be found dressing or even showering. Emerging from his bath he would begin searching for us and realize that we were already sitting in the car. Dressing and combing as fast as he could, he would then rush through the house, exit the garage and approach the driver's door. At this point, my mother would turn amazingly prophetic.

"Watch, kids," she would say, "he will have forgotten something!"

And sure enough, just as he reached for the handle to his door, Dad would check his pockets for wallet, comb, lighter, keys, or tickets, and, finding at least one of these missing, would dash back into the house. He never heard my mother's explosive "Punctuality Lecture," which as we matured admonished us never to be so thoughtless, irresponsible and discourteous as to make our hosts wait for us. We needed to plan ahead to assure that we arrived punctually, showing respect and appreciation for all the kindnesses our hosts were about to shower on us according to their careful strategic plan. By the time Dad returned to the car, Mom was finished with the Punctuality Lecture, so he never heard it. She was so angry that she would face her window, from the perspective of our back seat giving him a very obvious cold shoulder, which I realize now he never noticed. If we were destined for the home of one our Ukrainian relatives, we were always the first to arrive.

After leaving home, I called my parents every weekend and could always tell what kind of week it had been by my Mom's tone of voice. If she sounded discouraged, I'd have a good hunch what the problem was—it was a pretty safe bet that her frustration had been aroused by one of Dad's appointments with someone. I'd ask to speak with my father, a man of few words. A typical conversation went something like this:

"Hi, Dad."

"Hi, Michael."

"How are you?"

"Fine."

"Mom says you had a doctor's appointment this week."

"Yeah."

"She says you were late."

"Not really."

"Well, she told me that you were supposed to be there by 11 a.m. and that you arrived at 11:12."

"Yeah."

"Isn't that late?"

A long pause, and then Dad answers, "Not really."

"How do you figure that, Dad?"

And I would get his side of the story, his understanding of this aspect of the game of life as he had always understood and played it.

"The doctor never takes you at your appointed time. They always make you wait. The furniture is uncomfortable. The magazines are old and boring. The waiting room is filled with people infected with all kinds of dangerous microbes. Who wants to sit in a crowded, infected, overheated parlor with nothing to do for a half hour? If you show up 15 minutes 'late' (and you are 82 and standing there with your walker's support), they take you right in!"

Anyone who has had to wait to see their doctor under such conditions knows my father has the situation pretty well analyzed.

Is his "game" right or wrong, better or worse than my mother's? We can see that at least in terms of punctuality, it is different. One sees life as a timed event, governed by the clock; the other does not. In our household there were two ball games played on the same playing field with two different sets of rules. My parents were married 59 years, but never agreed on what it meant to be "on time."

When I moved to rural Alaska, I had no idea I was entering yet another ballpark. Among Tlingit people in Southeast Alaska, formal dinners—most often memorial feasts, known in Tlingit as "koo.éex'"—provide meaning and focus to their lives. Around the time I was first adopted into the Kaagwaantaan clan, I learned the clan would be responsible for hosting one of these events. I asked what time it was scheduled to start and appeared at the site "in plenty of time," as my Mom had taught me. All those Punctuality Lectures had their impact on my understanding of the game of life. But I soon discovered that my Tlingit friends defined "on time" yet another way. When they said "the feast will begin at 7 p.m.," it never meant "at exactly 7." Nor did it mean "Anytime after 7 will be fine." Their concept of on time was "sometime that evening, when conditions are ripe." And, in fact, the meal would seldom begin before nine. Their attitude seemed to be, "We'll start sometime that evening whenever most of the people show up, and the event will continue for the next three days, give or take a few hours, which are hardly significant in the total scheme of things."

DIFFERENT WORLDS, DIFFERENT VIEWS

Different cultures see the world differently. Different cultures structure, understand and play the game of life differently. These are not differences of right and wrong, good or bad, practical or impractical. They are just different, in the way baseball, football, basketball, hockey and tennis are different ball games. Comparisons do not equate with moral judgments. It is useful to understand what game you are playing before interacting regularly with another person. Otherwise, one risks playing a sort of "tackle basketball," in which both sides get annoyed, confused, frustrated or depressed.

We often assume that everyone understands and plays the game of life exactly as we play it, and it can come as a shock to realize that they don't. Initially this can lead to one group accusing the other of being incompetent, deceitful, rude or stupid. Whenever you are tempted to think that way about an individual or a group, consider the possibility that you may have just experienced another impromptu, unexpected round of "tackle basketball."

While thinking of cultures in terms of different ball games with different rules may be helpful when comparing two or more cultures that we don't belong to, this approach becomes less useful when we start to look at ourselves. Because we have been internalizing the rules and conventions of our own cultural ball games since infancy, when asked to outline the "game of life" as we understand and play it, none of us seem readily able to articulate the basic structure of our culture, the thousands of norms and rules that govern it, nor the ways players demonstrate competence or expertise on our playing field. While we know rationally as well as intuitively how to play the game we have been playing all of our lives, to write down all of its rules would be a tedious and formidable task. We may know how to play baseball well enough, but explaining it to the exchange student from Pakistan can prove frustratingly difficult.

So, while thinking of culture as the game of life as we understand and play it may help us gain a greater appreciation and tolerance for cultural differences, it does not help us much when it comes to reflecting upon or articulating anything very insightful about our own culture.

The following third approach may prove more helpful in defining one's own cultural identity. I arrived at it, I must confess, after reading a very challenging fantasy entitled *Ishmael*—the story of a wise gorilla who advertises in the classified section of a large metropolitan newspaper for a human being who desires to help save the world. An unemployed journalist applies for the position, subsequently entering telepathically into a conversation with Ishmael. The ape first instructs him to, "Bring me your myths." The journalist at first brings in Greek and Roman stories about gods and goddesses, which Ishmael summarily rejects. The journalist then comes back with the sacred texts of the major religions of the world, which Ishmael also refuses. When, after several more false starts, the newsman protests, "Explain to me what you want!" the gorilla answers, "Your myths are the stories you tell yourself about how things got to be the way they are."

"Oh," says the human, "you mean science, astronomy, chemistry and biology!"

"That's what you call them," replies the ape. "From a gorilla's perspective, those are your myths!"

"No," the human protests. "Those are the facts. Science is true!"

The great ape and the man go on to get into a long debate, but for our purposes the gorilla's initial point is valid. Myths are the stories we tell ourselves about how things got to be the way they are. And culture is the enactment of those myths. Another way of defining culture, then, is the "enactment of your story."

None of our stories began at birth, but long before that blessed event. Our grandparents or great grandparents wrote the first chapter. Their offspring wrote the next. You and I are at least chapter three in the story, and our children and grandchildren will continue the saga.

FAMILY STORIES

Using Ishmael's approach, to know my own "culture," I must be able to recognize my own stories. How did my family get to be the way it is? How and where did my grandparents meet? What were their childhoods, adolescence and adult lives like? What were their trials and triumphs? What major crises and obstacles did they overcome to make possible the life I entered into at birth? What stories have been passed down through the generations about the ancestors that ultimately have influenced who I am? Into what kind of story was I born? Something highly dramatic? Movingly tragic? Upliftingly comic? Or excitingly adventurous? Who were the main characters in chapters one and two of the family story, before I came along? You are the continuation of an ongoing story, whether you know it or not.

I remember only one story about my mother's maternal grandfather, Henry Dorn, and know only a few things about him. My mom said that he was scarred and often bruised, a little man of about five feet, thin and wiry, who worked as a blacksmith on the borders of Pennsylvania's Amish country. She remembers witnessing in horror more than once her little grandpa jettisoned out of his barn and crashing onto the flagstone pavement in front of it, having been kicked hard by one of his customers. But he would always arise slowly, dust himself off, pick up his hammer, and charge back into the barn to finish shoeing that horse or mule. That is the full unabridged story I heard more than once in childhood. My sister recalls the flying blacksmith story as well. Neither of us can now recall why we were told this family myth, but we have a hunch.

There are situations in every young person's life when he or she decides things have not worked out as expected. Having launched a career as a concert violinist or professional ballplayer with much enthusiasm, once the practices wear on, the assignments become more difficult, the routine less inviting, it is only natural to want out. "I don't want to do this anymore!" Or "This is too hard!" Or "I'm not having fun!" Or "I can't!"—the refrain heard most frequently around our house growing up. Times like these mom would sit us down and tell us the blacksmith story. The moral was clear: "You don't come from a family of quitters. My grandfather did not necessarily enjoy being catapulted into the barnyard, but that pain and humiliation never stopped him from getting the job done. You come from a line of determined, stubborn people. Giving up is not an option. Get back to work!" Even as I write these words, an ancient unsmiling photo of that great grandpa looks down on me, and I realize my own life will make up the next chapter in his story.

There is a larger and happier portrait displayed above that of Henry Dorn in my office—the pleasant and approving face of my Dad's mother, Anna. Unlike the blacksmith I never met, I knew her well. For half a century, all major holidays were celebrated at her house. Most of the family gathered there on Sundays after church for a delicacy we named BBCs—Baba's Breakfast Cakes—and coffee or milk. As a teen, I would linger for hours researching the story of her childhood in rural Ukraine—a place that seemed to me like another world. And it was.

Baba was the oldest of ten children, born in the section of the Carpathian Mountains not far from Sanok, in what today is southeastern Poland. Fruit trees stood in front of each house, and fields of wheat and vegetables extended out back, occupied by chickens, ducks, geese, a few turkeys, sheep, pigs, and usually one cow. These were peasant farmers, living off of land they had occupied for centuries. Their plots and livestock provided all their immediate needs. Their woolen clothing was woven from yarn they had spun themselves, their shoes made of leather they had tanned, or in some cases the tree bark they had gathered. Their homes were clay brick and thatch. While life was never what we today would call comfortable, famine was rare. Although cash was an uncommon luxury, villagers subsisted well enough on what they could sow and harvest for themselves.

The village had a few literate leaders. The mayor read aloud to everyone within earshot the new decrees sent out from government headquarters, to be certain folks stayed current on any new rules. The priest chanted the appointed daily scriptural readings and celebrated with his flock a fourth century liturgy that the locals knew by heart in the ancient Slavonic translation. The postmaster not only sold stamps, but read mail aloud to illiterate recipients, took dictation, and addressed and stamped replies, charging a small fee for his combined services.

These were the most highly respected leaders in the community, all of whom had acquired their status by virtue of being able to read. There was no building called "school," but a system of itinerant teachers called "shkola." Similar to the way piano teachers might come to a suburban house today, these instructors traveled from village to village offering their services for hire. Those with money would invite them into their home for several-hour lessons in reading, writing, arithmetic, and often religion. Rabbis would come around to prepare Jewish children for their Bar Mitzvahs. (My grandmother remembers learning how to read a few Hebrew words when she sat in on a few such lessons).

Anna's dad did not have money, so she never attended one day of shkola. It was her great regret that she never learned to read, nor to write more than her own name.

One day her father approached Anna with a request. Her mother's three sisters had gone to this far off place called America, and they were inviting her to join them there. They were earning good salaries, and, if Anna were willing to cross the ocean, would welcome her into their boarding house and secure a similar factory job for her. This way, she could send money home and significantly improve the living standard for her family. *Was she willing to go to America?* Hardly aware of how distant this land was, totally unable to grasp how momentous this decision would be, my grandmother agreed. A year later she was on a train, passing through Poland and Germany, boarding a ship in Hamburg bound for New York City.

Once when I was a teen, my father took my mother, my sister, my brother, my grandmother and me to visit the Statue of Liberty. I recall standing at the base of Miss Liberty and hearing my grandmother telling us about her arrival a half-century earlier. The ship, she said, passed through the channel to the right and landed at the island to the left. The Ellis Island immigration station—then a derelict mansion, its windows smashed and roof partly collapsed—welcomed tens of millions of Europeans to the New World at the end of the nineteenth century. Baba joined us in our ascent of the statue, climbing the hundreds of stairs inside. I don't recall if she made it to the windows at the top that constitute Liberty's crown. But I know on that day my grandmother's arrival in America found a place in the story I carry of my family.

Thirty years later, I picked up another piece. Myths are like that; you seldom get the whole story all at once. Instead, we pick up parts of our huge historical jigsaw puzzle here and there, and fit them together one piece at a time. And there always seem to be pieces missing. (I never asked, for example, how Baba managed to get on the right trains or find the right ship when everything would have been written in Polish and German as she traveled west).

Several years ago, my grandmother and I were walking together to visit the grave of my grandfather, who had collapsed and died suddenly at the age of 32 in their farmhouse in Macungie, Pennsylvania. At the time of this visit to her husband's grave, my grandmother had been a widow for over sixty years. Walking slightly ahead of me, she stopped suddenly, turned halfway around, and spoke to me in a thick Slavic accent: "You know, Michael, I marry you gran'fodder because he promise to take me home!" She took a few more steps and just as suddenly stopped again, adding, "And then... he died! The bum!"

Years before, she had told me how homesick she had been after arriving in America—how unhappy she was and unsatisfying she found the routine of the factory to be. She missed her parents, her village and the rural life there. She had met and married John Oleksa here—they planned to save enough money to return to the Ukraine, but the trip never happened. The First World War, the Russian Revolution and Civil War, then the birth of their first child all forced postponement of their plans until their dream evaporated. When my grandfather passed away, my grandmother was left with four little children and only a small farm to sustain them.

She once told me how the state police appeared one morning at her farmhouse door. With some apprehension she invited them inside, where they began immediately to scold her in English—a language she could barely understand. "Mrs. Oleksa!" they began, "you are in violation of the Commonwealth of Pennsylvania's compulsory school attendance law!" Unable to comprehend most of what they were saying, when they repeated, "School! School, Mrs. Oleksa! Your children belong in school!" Baba finally understood. "Ah! Shkola!"

Momentarily excusing herself, she retreated to her bedroom and returned, holding open an empty purse to show the officers that she had no cash to pay for lessons. Her children could not attend school. "No," the policemen explained. "You do not need to pay. You do not need money. In America we require all children to go to school, but it is free." I have no idea how those troopers communicated this revolutionary idea to my grandmother. I am certain that they spoke no Ukrainian and she spoke no English.

After they eventually managed to somehow convey their meaning to her, she was astounded. "Let me get this straight. In

America, all kids must go to school, but the parents do not have to send money for each lesson? In America," she repeated, "children must get an education and it is provided free of charge?" Still dumbfounded, she reiterated, "In this land, all the young people receive instruction at no cost? Shkola is free? What a country!"

I wish I had a videotape of this conversation.

The next morning, my aunt and father became the first Oleksas in history to be sent to school. Before they left the house, Baba had a few encouraging words for them. Her lecture began like this: "You children are so lucky to be born in America. If we had gone back to Europe, as your father and I had planned, there would be no shkola for you. You would be unable to read or write, like me. But here, they require you to attend school. They make you get an education. And you don't even have to pay for it!"

Still overwhelmed by this amazing and unexpected blessing, she continued, "So you better take advantage of this. Respect your teachers. Listen to everything they tell you. Do your best work. Try hard to learn." Turning to my father, she added, "And don't disgrace us!" Wagging her finger before him she warned, "If I find out you were fooling around, if I find out you got into trouble, if I find out you had to be disciplined for breaking the rules there...." and she took a breath, "I'm warning you now: whatever punishment they dole out there, when you get home, it will be much worse!"

Now, how do I know this lecture so well, when it was delivered in Ukrainian decades before my birth? You can guess. Yes, I heard the whole story at the dinner table—the night before I left home for kindergarten. And so did all ten of my cousins.

That's the "story into which we were born." Let's look at its impact from a cultural standpoint. We were all expected to do well in school. Our grandmother had always wanted an education but never had the opportunity. Two of her four children managed, against all odds, to earn their high school diplomas. That the grandchildren were going to go to college had been determined before any of us were born. And we did. Baba proudly attended all the high school graduation ceremonies and then all the college commencement ceremonies. We knew how pleased she was. She once commented, "I have thirteen grandchildren and there's not a bum among them!" Only John Oleksa had been assigned that status!

No one possesses the final or complete version of the Family Myth. Different offspring hear different stories or versions of stories, each edited specifically to make whatever point an elder or parent needed to make at the time it was told.

TIMELESS TIME

Every culture offers unique insights into the human condition and brings forth a unique perspective, a "beam of light" along which a particular people views the world. In this sense, there is no such thing as a "little" or insignificant culture. One cannot judge the value or importance of a language or culture by the number of its speakers or members, any more than one can judge the significance of a person by his or her height.

The modern world has become sensitive to the plight of animal species threatened by extinction in the face of humanity's dramatic expansion across the globe. But we have yet to develop a sense of cultural ecology that expresses a similar concern for the destruction of irreplaceable worldviews, embodied in the stories and values of traditional societies. These, too, are threatened with disruption, assimilation, and, in some cases, annihilation. Thus, far from being mere fables from a bygone era, the "old stories" bring with them into the present day ways of looking along a unique beam of light that no one else has noticed.

Understood as the tradition bearers understand them, the stories about Beginnings in particular become windows that offer a view into another world or a unique view of this one. Knowledge of the eternal patterns and structures contained in the old stories frames the foundation and focus of the education of a Human Being in a tribal culture. Then it becomes absolutely essential for the younger generation to apply this information to their own lives, for them to live in accordance with the paradigms and models revealed in those ancient tales, avoiding the mistakes and disastrous consequences of violating them, as portrayed in the stories.

When a teen conforms to these standards and structures, he is acting appropriately, the way a Real Person should. But more, he is placing himself in harmony and solidarity with his ancestors, acting as they acted, behaving as they behaved. His behavior is not innovative, an expression of his own individual and creative character, but a ritual action he did not invent. Like the expectant Yup'ik mother (discussed in the Yup'ik chapter) who deliberately bows her head and exits head first, without stopping, the boy who moves, acts, speaks, hunts, fishes, butchers, shares, cooks, cleans and disposes of the leftovers (like the muskrat bones) does none of these according to his own imagination. Rather, he does as the People have always done, since "those days." He lives "as we always do"—meaning as members of his traditional society have lived since the Beginning of Time.

This concept, perhaps the most complex in this book, may be a little difficult to grasp, since English does not have words adequate to convey these experiences. When a language does not have a word for something, this indicates that people in that culture do not have this experience or perception.

Greek is the only European language that shared the sense of time I am about to describe. The ancient Hellenes had two words for time. The first, as I mentioned earlier, is "Chronos." From this Greek word we get our own words "chronology" and "chronological," for sequential time—time that moves from moment to moment, hour to hour, day to day, week to week, month to month, year to year. Chronos moves irreversibly forward. It flows like a river, drains like grains of sand in an hourglass. This is the only sense of time generally understood in modern culture. What's more, we take very seriously this "chronological" aspect of the "game of life" as we play it. We take courses in "Time Management," conceptualizing the Chronos of our lives and of the world as a valuable commodity we can "lose," "gain," or even "save."

Other earlier cultures also experienced time as moving forever forward, from day to day and year to year; but there was another kind of time, which the Greeks called Kairos (Keh-ROS). A person enters Kairos deliberately, consciously, on purpose. Kairos is possible only when there is an ancient model or paradigm to be replicated, to be made present again. There must be a formula to be repeated, a ritual to be enacted in order to enter Kairos. When a person does something, anything, according to an ancient pattern, a pattern revealed in the sacred stories, the time spent performing that action is no longer Chronos, but Kairos. Kairos is Chronos made into something else, transformed into meaningful, sacred time. Kairos can be invoked even in the modern world.

A Jewish family sitting down to a ritual Passover Feast, the Seder, and opening the Haggadah (the book containing the instructions, prayers and hymns for the evening), is entering Kairos. Participants in the Seder do not invent the menu, nor the sequence of actions. They perform the actions and recite the prayers, many of them in Hebrew (whether or not they speak or understand this language), "the way we always have," since the first Passover, thousands of years ago. The youngest son chants the Four Questions, though they are not personally his questions. He reads them or has memorized them from the text.

I remember the first time I participated in a Seder and watched my friends perform the meal. I had never been part of such an intricate ritual meal before and had to read all the fine print in the Haggadah to know what to do next. Raise the glass. Dip the matzoh. Eat some bitter herbs. A process made even more complicated because the Haggadah is read back to front.

The summer following my first Passover Seder, I got a job at a summer camp operated by the Jewish Community Center in my hometown. In the winter I was invited to work indoors at their winter camp during the December holiday, Hannukah. During that time I learned a lot more about Jewish culture and the Hebrew language, so that the next spring, when I was once again invited to celebrate Passover, I was much better prepared. As the youngest male child at the table, it was my task to pose the Four Questions, which I sang, much to the delight of my hosts, in Hebrew.

Doing something "the way we always do" puts a person into the sunbeam. Instead of looking at the light, as I had when I first attended the Seder, the second year I could look along it, participate in it.

Chronos is the time we spend looking at something from the outside; Kairos is the time we spend participating in something from the inside. Whenever we do, we put ourselves in solidarity with those who also are performing this action, not only in this particular place at this particular moment, but throughout the world, across all geographic boundaries, and throughout history, across all barriers of time.

When, at the festal table, I chanted the Four Questions in Hebrew, I did what every Jewish boy that night had done whenever they were the youngest son at their Seder. I did what the youngest son at every table was doing that night at every Seder. I did what every boy not yet born would do when it became his duty at some future Seder. The questions were not my questions. The language was not my language. But when I sang "Why is this night different from all other nights...?" I put myself deliberately, consciously, in solidarity with all those sons throughout time—past, present and future—on purpose. That is Kairos. Kairos is born of Tradition.

But there is another aspect of Kairos that perhaps is its most complex. It may best be explained through the following example from Christianity. Kairos requires the repetition of a paradigmatic act. For Christians, this is most obviously the Lord's Supper, the Eucharist.

In an upper room in Jerusalem about two thousand years ago, Jesus of Nazareth took bread and broke it, blessed the cup and offered it to his disciples. Certain words were said over certain food. And whenever Christians gather and repeat those same words over that same food, whatever the Apostles received that night, there, "in those days," is identical to what the believer receives now. Repeat the words and actions and you are there, no sci-fi time machine needed. Kairos not only remembers the sacred words or actions of that long ago time, Kairos is the possibility of participating in the sacred event of "that time"—because, as sacred, it is eternally accessible. The Sacred Event is eternally "open." No one can be late for the Last Supper.

These examples from contemporary religious life share similarities with the way traditional people live, not only in their spiritual life, but at all times. While experiencing Chronos, they also tend to view it as fundamentally meaningless. Their great desire is to transform it into Kairos, meaningful time; to escape the "burden" of history, the time that moves from a beginning to an unavoidable end, and to make possible a return to the ideal—the beautiful time of the Beginning, when the world was new and human beings dwelt in paradise. In the Alaskan stories of the beginnings of the world, the earth is always warm, the air still, the sun shining, the animals kind and cooperative. This is the Arctic Eden.

Unlike the limited experience of Kairos in modern society, traditional cultures like the Athabascans seek to live in Kairos as much of the time as possible. There are stories and therefore patterns indicating how Human Beings should perform dozens of daily actions. There are rules governing how mundane or burdensome chores should be done. There is the right way to leave the house, the right way to skin a beaver, the right way to take out the garbage. Necessary though not necessarily pleasant work is transformed into a sacred task by means of a story that provides the appropriate model. The time spent executing this action is no longer sequential, chronological time measured by the clock; it is a moment of meaningful, cyclical time measured in eternity. It is Kairos. Timeless time.

Inupiat dancer. *Photo by Bill Hess*

Preceding page: Women of a Tununak family distribute a young man's first bearded seal.

Top: A family picking salmonberries near Kotlik.

Bottom: Toksook Bay seal hunters study ice conditions.

Photos by James H. Barker

THE REAL PEOPLE

When we use the phrase "Yup'ik people," we are actually being redundant. Most traditional tribes call themselves "the Human Beings," or "the People," and the Eskimo, Amerindian and Aleuts of Alaska are no exception. The word for the main indigenous group in the Alaskan Panhandle, the Tlingit, means "the People." The various Athabascan tribes of the interior and southcentral regions call themselves "Dineh," "Dene," "Dena'ina," or some variant of these, all of which translate to "the People," or "the Humans." Yup'ik or Inupiaq go a step further, however. Their names translate to "the Real People."

There are, the Yup'ik tell us, imposters out there. Human wannabees. And one of the first lessons every traditional child must learn is how to distinguish between "us" and "them." The Real People act the way Human Beings should, as the Creator taught the First People "ak'a tamaani," in the old days, a long time ago.

All cultures, including the Yup'ik, carry forward stories about their origins. According to the Yup'ik story of the Beginning, the first humans emerged from pods of beach grass. These creatures came as something of a surprise to the Creator, (a Raven, as is often the case in Alaskan creation stories), who came strolling along that beach and discovered the First Man and the First Woman.

"What sort of creature are you?" Raven asked, somewhat perplexed. "Not enough fur and no feathers! Pitiful! Pathetic! Doomed!"

But Raven felt a little sorry for these featherless, fangless, clawless creatures, so he assembled all the Arctic animals for consultation. "Look at these weird new creatures I've discovered. They have no chance of survival in this land. Once winter arrives they'll die of starvation or hypothermia. Any suggestions?"

The animals all took pity on the First People and offered to help them. The Human Beings (Yuut) and the other Living Things (Ungungsiit) entered into a covenant. The Animals would offer themselves to the human hunters, who could use their skins as clothing in the cold Alaskan winter, and consume their flesh as food. In return, the Animals demanded respect, gratitude and an attitude of humility from the People. As long as the People treated the Animals respectfully and approached them without arrogance or indifference, the Animals would sacrifice themselves so that the Humans could survive.

To this day, it is the duty of every human being, young and old alike, to honor this covenant. Violation of it can result in catastrophe.

Interestingly, this sort of bilateral agreement is common among hunting peoples throughout the world. Recognizing their dependence on the animals for survival, hunters often acknowledge their inability to catch any prey that does not offer itself to them. The animals, they recognize, are smart. They see what humans cannot see. They hear what humans cannot hear. They smell what humans cannot detect. And they are in cahoots. They share their information between species, so that if the moose, for example, with his big nose and big ears does not smell or hear a human approaching, the sparrow will alert him. People cannot ever surprise, outsmart, or overpower their prey. They only catch those animals that make themselves available. And the animals offer themselves only to humble and grateful people who observe the appropriate gestures and rites of respect. This covenant with the animals lies at the heart of Yup'ik culture to the present era.

I did not grow up in a hunting tradition. My father never hunted, although his father did, in the forests near their Pennsylvania farmhouse. We still keep his shotgun, now an antique, as an heirloom and reminder of the last Oleksa hunter. I had no personal experience of hunting until I was invited to a Yup'ik village over three decades ago. My former high school students not only invited me to their hometown, but took me on my first hunting trip, by boat, along the shores of the flooded Kuskokwim River in southwestern Alaska.

It was May. As we left Kwethluk that morning, snow fell gently across the landscape and the sloughs were still bound in ice. I do not recall my guides discussing any particular prey or saying explicitly which animal they were seeking. I recognize now that may have been part of the etiquette. Talking about the animals as if you knew which one might offer itself to you could be tempting fate, behaving arrogantly. It is not up to humans, but up to the animals, which food will be provided and when.

So off we went, as if simply on a boat ride, rifles at the ready, just in case. Ultimately we came home with about a dozen muskrats. With the ice jam in the river, the temporary lake that flooded these little mammals' homeland for miles in all directions left them no place to alight. Exhausted after swimming for days, they seemed to give themselves up to us gladly, fulfilling their part in the ancient bargain.

We returned to the village and to the one-room log cabin that was my primary home that month. The lady of the house was delighted with the muskrats, quickly skinning them and placing their tiny hides on willow stretchers. A few more dozen of these would be enough for a nice winter parka. The meat was cooked in the most typical Yup'ik way. I tease my wife—I met her along the shores of that ice-jammed lake that same spring—that her people's cookbook always begins with the instruction, "Boil water." Eskimos prefer soup.

This particular evening, my hostess and cook alerted me that I did not have to join in the muskrat feast. There was, she noted, a sufficient supply of peanut butter and jelly somewhere nearby and I could substitute a less exotic menu. "No," I replied. "Yupiaruunga!" I am a Real Person! She smiled and nodded, then invited some elders to join us for dinner.

Yup'ik communities are what anthropologists call "high context" places. This means that people assume a lot of things about each other that people in other cultures probably would not. They assume that their neighbors know them pretty well, recognize the sound of their voices, and therefore do not need to identify themselves on the telephone, a recently introduced technology in most villages. They know that their neighbors have visited their houses for many years and know where they keep things. They

Preparing a seal in Alakanuk. *Photo by James H. Barker*

know that anyone is welcome at their table any time. So a guest entering a house and finding the family enjoying supper will wordlessly proceed directly to the appropriate cupboard, remove a plate or bowl, help himself to a serving, sit down, and, without any verbal interchange, join the household at dinner, finish his meal, and leave—oftentimes without saying a single word. And that's what is considered a visit! Among Real People, silence really is golden.

Another aspect of this high value on quiet is the reluctance to discuss or explain verbally. Children learn by watching adults and mimicking them, rather than by receiving explicit verbal explanations or warnings.

As I sat down to my first muskrat dinner, I was about to learn some fundamental principles of Yup'ik etiquette without anybody telling me anything. Rather than being expected to get up and help ourselves at the stove, we visitors were invited to the table and told to sit down. The meal was brought to us by the cook, as if she were a waitress in a diner. Prior to the meal, moistened washcloths were positioned strategically around the table. Each place setting consisted of a single soup spoon. As dinner was served, a few things seemed peculiar to me. Although each bowl contained broth and vegetables—an assortment of onions, carrots, potatoes, and rice—its principal occupant was one skinned and gutted, tailless muskrat, paws and toothy smile intact, sort of sitting there looking at me. I was somewhat taken aback by this presentation, but said nothing.

My host, a former student just a few years younger than me, delighted in initiating me into his culture. Smiling broadly and pointing emphatically at my bowl, he whispered repeatedly into my ear, "Rats! Rats! You're eating rats!" I did my best to ignore him; he was eating the same meal after all. And besides, I persuaded myself, I have no idea what they put into hot dogs either! It was impossible to eat the muskrat with the single utensil I had been given. The elders who had been invited (in retrospect it seems obvious to show me by their example how to proceed) dove their hands directly into their soup, removing chunks of tasty meat from the muskrat carcass. I did my best to imitate them.

After about a half-hour the hostess approached me with a predictable question. "Taquten-qaa?" she asked. (You're finished, aren't you?) "Ii-yi." I replied, thinking I really had had enough. She did not say anything but her facial expression conveyed some concern if not disapproval. This woman was my primary Yup'ik language teacher and whenever I answered correctly she nodded enthusiastically and smiled. Now there was no sign of either. I quickly changed my mind. "Taqsaitua," I said, reversing myself. "I'm not done yet!" She put my bowl back on the table and moved away.

The problem was I didn't know why I was not supposed to be finished yet. Meanwhile, those elders were still busy at it. Carefully removing every shred of muskrat meat, they spent a lot of time noisily inhaling the scraps that remained on the bones. When they were finished, there was nothing left but a polished muskrat skeleton. In the history of Kentucky Fried Chicken, Colonel Sanders never saw the likes of this. I did my best to imitate these elders, though I was far less proficient. In time the cook returned and repeated her question. "Nutaan-qaa taq'uten?" (Now you're finished, aren't you?) Somewhat less confident this second time, I answered "Ii-yi." And with a broad smile and an emphatic nod she exclaimed "Ii-yi!" I had discovered the cardinal principle of Yup'ik etiquette: waste nothing.

I later learned that those tiny bones, the remnants of the muskrat, for which I assumed humans had no use, would be returned to the pond from which the muskrat had come. As the hunter places the bones into the water, often through the ice, he says, "Cali taikina!" (Come back!) If the People have treated these animals appropriately, if they have spoken of them with respect, hunted, killed, skinned and cooked, eaten and handled even the leftovers with respect, muskrats will return to give themselves once more to the Human Beings.

On the other hand, if any of the protocols are broken, the entire community can suffer from the refusal of these and other animals to offer themselves to them as food and clothing. The whole town and every resident must follow this covenant. When the bones are returned to their home, the spirits of the muskrats who have given themselves, and the spirits of those who survive, are appeased. They see that their sacrifice was appreciated. In making this gesture of gratitude, proving that the fur and flesh were fully and appropriately utilized, the humans are behaving in a respectful and humble way. To put the bones back into the pond with meat still on them would be to say, "You died for nothing. We took your meat and threw it away." Insulted in this way, muskrats would not again offer themselves to such ungrateful creatures.

The Yup'ik Story that follows takes place on a particular stage, a Yup'ik cosmos constructed of several levels. The earth sits in the middle of this universe, as a flat saucer floating in a bowl with a domed lid over it. The dome has a hole in its center, the passage to the world beyond. Each level has a name: the earth is called Nuna (noo-NAH), the dome of the sky Qilak (kee-LAHK), and the underworld Imaq (ee-MAHK). The First People believed that this view of the world's structure, given to them when they originally emerged, provides the blueprint for their homes. Every house is built in the image of the universe. Every home is a microcosm, a miniature world.

The way the Yup'ik view the organization of the universe also explains certain behaviors that might not at first make much sense to an outside observer.

My Yup'ik wife, Xenia, and I have four adult children. (I like to call them Eskirainians or Ukrainiamos, which makes my grandsons with Norwegian and Aleut ancestry "Scandaleuyupikra iniamos"!) Because Xenia carried our first child, Anastasia, during the warmest and brightest months of the year, I was too busy to notice her pregnancy rituals. Our second daughter, Ekatrina, was born in late January, though, and since the months that Xenia was carrying her were among the coldest and darkest, I was around more to observe my wife's peculiar behavior during her pregnancy.

Though I knew her not to be a "morning person," I noticed that during her pregnancy Xenia was getting up early, washing, dressing and leaving the house, no matter what the weather. Wondering why she was repeatedly getting up early to go out into the dark, cold, snow-driven morning, one day I decided to ask her about it. "Is there something traditionally Yup'ik about what you're doing? Getting up early and leaving the house?" From her facial expression I could tell my question had surprised her, but she just answered matter-of-factly, "Yes." The tone of her voice was like, "Well, of course!" While I was looking at her culture, she was looking along it. I decided to drop the line of questioning and went on about my business still wondering about her ritual.

Six months later, I was invited to deliver a commencement address at a boarding school on the Yukon River. I arrived by plane and threw my baggage into a dormitory room, then hurried to the nearby cafeteria for supper. As soon as I sat down with my tray, a half dozen Real People surrounded me. They were students from the senior class who would be graduating the next day, and each was eager to determine if this alien could really talk like a Human Being.

"Kituusit?" their leader, Ben, asked.

Kina is the Yup'ik word for Who? The endings attached here (–uu and –sit?) translate as "are" and "you," singular and interrogative. I told them my Yup'ik name,

"Atertayagaq."

Aterte- is the stem of the verb "to drift" and the ending "yagaq" means "the little one who___". So my name means "the Little Drifter," and I live up to it, having dwelt in a dozen different towns across the southern half of Alaska during my 35 years here.

So far, so good, I thought. I was passing my Human Being exam. Ben continued, "Camiungusit?"

This construction was a little more complicated. "Ca" means "What?" The ending " – miu" means a resident or citizen of a place, plus the question endings, "are" and "you?" The concept is, "What (place) are you a resident/citizen of?" or, as we might say in English, "Where are you from?" I couldn't claim to have been born in the Yup'ik region, or to be a citizen of what one of our visitors from Canada named "Yupikia," so I answered truthfully,

"Aipaqa Kuigllugmiunguq."

"Aipa" is spouse or companion, and adding the " –qa" meant "my spouse." Kuiglluk (literally, "Bad River") is her hometown, so my response would translate "My wife is from Kwethluk."

I was batting two for two, and starting to feel fairly confident. Then they asked,

"Naken anellruusit?"

I understood these words grammatically, but it was obvious we were looking along some different sunbeam at this point. "Na–" is the base word for "where?" Nani means "in where?" Natmun means "to where?" Naken means "from where?" "Ane-" is the verb for to exit, to go out. "An'ua" means "I'm going out," or "I'm exiting." "I want to go out" would be "Anyugtua." I don't want to go out, "Anyuumiitua." You probably don't want to go out would be translated, "Anyuumiicugnarquten." You get the idea. The way Real People talk (Yugtun, "like people") requires the accumulation of more and more endings to further modify the original concept.

I had grasped this fundamental principle years earlier, but there was no way for me to make sense of this question, "From where did you exit?"

The last place I had exited was the dormitory. Although I still didn't really understand the question, I ventured an answer. "Inarvigmek." I came out of the dorm.

It was obvious from the expression on the faces of these teen interrogators that I had just flunked my test. They glanced at each other both puzzled and amused. So I asked them to repeat the question. They did, the way people everywhere do when they sense there has been some misunderstanding, slower and louder—as if this were the key to clear communication.

"NAKEN ANEllruuSIT?," they shouted in unison.

I was still stumped. I went back one frame and answered "Tengssuutemek."

"Teng– " is the verb for flying and "– ssuun" is the ending for "a machine used for __," so Tengssuun is a machine used for flying—an airplane. That was the last thing, besides the dormitory, I could recall exiting. The students looked at each other incredulous, wordlessly expressing the impossibility of this response. My answer did not compute. Finally I surrendered. "Taringesciigaatamci!" I can't understand you guys.

So they switched immediately to English: "Where were you born?" Well, not in the dorm or the plane, that was for sure!

I returned home to continue my inquiry into my wife's prenatal behavior.

"I know I asked you this before, Dear," I began, "but is there something particular you do when you go outside during your pregnancies? Is there some special way you have to exit or some ritual action you perform when you go out each morning?"

With the same *Of course! Doesn't everyone know this already?* sort of expression, she answered, "Yes!"

"Well could you explain to me what that is?" I pleaded.

"Well, when a Yup'ik mother-to-be goes out each morning, she must be careful to pass through the door head first and without stopping. Head first and never pause in the actual passageway. Never put an arm or a leg through the doorway. Never back out. Always deliberately bend forward slightly and be certain that the head comes out first. And don't stop there. Keep going.

Now what was she (and every Real Mother before her) doing? I considered the shape of the traditional house, the image of the universe, and realized it was also shaped like the womb. How are healthy babies born? Head first and without stopping! That is not a pattern this mother discovered on her own, nor her mother or grandmother. This way of thinking went all the way back to the beginning. By conforming her behavior to those eternal structures and paradigms, the child will become a Real Person, a Human Being. Mothers are showing their children how to live even before they are born.

In the Yup'ik view, the idea of a birth being the child's "exiting" the mother, a process that could be facilitated by the way the mother exited her house during her pregnancy, was reflected in the word "exit" as the equivalent of the English "birth." This explained the strange inquiry of my students: "Where did you exit?"

It is at moments of intercultural communication breakdown like this that the possibility arises to see suddenly along the brilliance of another culture instead of looking at it. What feels like a problem can become a rich opportunity. The gap between people on either side of a cultural divide can become a means for entering another reality. Without the "hole" there is no entrance.

Stories provide the models, the eternal paradigms (patterns) for authentic human behavior, often by warning what may happen when you deviate from the right way. These tales reinforce admonitions by demonstrating potentially negative consequences: this is what you should do, and this is what happens if you disregard this norm.

Some stories contain within them songs that forever are identified with that particular tale. Other stories have inspired songs and dances. Others serve as a source of images and designs sewn into parkas and painted into bowls and spoons, and scrimshawed onto knives and harpoons. Art, music, song, dance, ceremony, and story constitute a holistic, integrated vision of the world. They are the visible, tangible expressions of how Real People see the world—their way of conveying the beam of light that contains the particles of this universe.

One final, fundamental principle of the Yup'ik world view is the concept of "Yua," literally "its person," "its personality," or even "its soul." This mysterious life or life-sustaining presence resides in all things. Traditionally, the Yup'ik, like many others, perceived this life force to be identical to the life within them, depicting it as human. When Raven lifts his beak or mask, he becomes what he really is, a human figure. The inner reality of other creatures is the same as ours. In Yup'ik art, the Yua is a human form embedded within the animal or spirit figure. A wooden mask representing a wolf, a seal, a whale, or a bear will look like a streamlined, elegant animal, but one of its eyes may be carved as an entire human face. That is the "Yua" of the creature, the life force, sacred and mysterious within it, identical to the life force in people.

Painted on a ladle or dish, a Yua may at first glance appear to represent a human figure inside the animal, as if a human had been eaten, but this is a misunderstanding. The human image within the caribou is its life force. And this life, wherever it is encountered, must be treated respectfully, reverently. The Yup'ik culture pivots on this essential idea, this way of understanding and relating to the natural world, including other Human Beings. Symbols such as Yua instruct that there is no barrier between human and animal, between "in here" and "out there," between self and other.

The Yup'ik seek ways in which to unite themselves with each other, building invisible networks of relationships where in other cultures none would exist. This is done most deliberately in the naming of children. The language and culture are gender-blind. There are no pronouns for he/she, nor possessive pronouns, his/her. Names are not associated with either gender; no names are reserved exclusively for boys or girls. When a respected elder dies in one village, the next several boys and girls in that or a neighboring town will often be named after that deceased person.

I initially encountered this as another one of those "gaps" between my world and the Yup'ik universe. Sitting in a home where a newborn baby girl was dozing in her cradle, I witnessed an elderly widow enter the house, approach the child, and, leaning over the railing, say to her, "How's my husband today?" I was tempted to think that granny had lost her sense of reality. This little girl cannot be her husband! Not in my world! But I said nothing. I long before had discovered that it is usually better to watch and listen than to ask too many questions, demand too many explanations.

An hour later, a middle-aged man came into the house, bent over the cradle and said to the infant girl, "How's my Daddy today?" I was feeling a little like I'd fallen through Alice's Rabbit Hole, into a very curious Wonderland. Is everyone going crazy? Right behind this man came his teenage daughter, who approached the child gleefully and exclaimed, "How beautiful you are, Grandpa!"

"Can someone explain to me," I asked quietly, "what is going on here? Why are all these visitors calling that little baby girl their husband, father and Ap'a?"

"Oh," said the new mother, "we gave her the name of that widow's departed spouse. She has that name." This gave a new and unexpected meaning to the phrase "in the name of . . ." The parents of the infant named their child after a recently deceased and highly respected elder and now their family is related to the widow and her family. The widow will call that little girl "my spouse" and her children will call her "our father" and the grandchildren will address her as "Grandpa" forever. They will give her extra gifts on her birthday and at Christmas, and make a fuss over her whenever they meet.

These families are now joined, and, as such, the parents will provide support for the widow. Later that summer I saw them take a boatload of salmon to the widow's fish camp. While unloading the salmon, they exclaimed "Your husband sends you these!"

In the Yup'ik world, everyone is related to everyone, one way or another. The very grammar of the Yup'ik language reinforces this conception of the universe. All the parts of each Yup'ik word (which, again, is more like an English sentence) need to relate appropriately to whatever comes before and after it. If necessary, the form will be altered to accommodate whatever surrounds it. Words, like people, seldom stand alone. Each must relate appropriately to its total environment.

When I first arrived in the Kuskokwim-Yukon Delta, the heartland of "Yupikia," I was introduced to Akutaq (ah-KOO-tahk), "Eskimo ice cream," a dessert made of whipped shortening, sugar and wild berries. Sitting at the table with my former students I noticed that I alone had been given a spoon with which to eat, while the others were using their fingers.

"Why am I eating with a spoon?" I asked.

"Because you're a Kass'aq (White Man)," they replied, smiling and laughing.

"Kass'aunritua!" *I'm no white guy!*, I exclaimed in protest, much to their delight. "Yupiaruunga!" *I'm a Real Person!* And I secretly promised myself never to use a spoon again when being offered akutaq.

Three months later, I visited another village to attend a conference at which only one other non-Yup'ik was present—an Aleut man from the island of St. George. He was both the keynote speaker and guest of honor at the concluding banquet. Seated at the far end of the head table, I received several huge bowls of akutaq, which I passed down to those seated nearby. I then took samples of each variety and began eating my dessert in the traditional way, with my fingers. Suddenly the elder sitting next to me nudged me with his foot.

"Michael!" he whispered in a scolding tone. "Use your spoon!"

I smiled at him and replied, "I know how to eat akutaq the Yup'ik way. Kassaunritua! I'm a Real Person!"

"Yes," he acknowledged pleasantly, but pointing toward the guest of honor at the middle of the head table he added, "but we have company!"

In deference to their honored visitor, I saw that all three hundred Yup'iks at the meal were using their spoons. I suspect none of them had to be kicked under the table to be reminded of their manners.

The Yup'ik universe is founded on the fundamental principle of harmonious relationships with all life—with the animals, with the spirits, with each other. Conflict should be avoided, peace restored, relationships strengthened—for it is only in unity with all others and indeed with all life that we become Real People, genuine Human Beings, Yup'iit.

Herring fishing near St. Michael on Norton Sound. *Photo by James H. Barker*

Hauling water from snowmelt at Umkumiut. *Photo by James H. Barker*

THE EYE OF THE NEEDLE

A TRADITIONAL YUP'IK TALE

There was once a grandmother who lived alone with her grandson in a traditional Yup'ik sod house, far away from any other dwelling. Dug partially into the ground, the basement or "imaq" of this sod house was used for storage. The imaq was built in the same form as the Imarpik, the real imaq, the sea. Driftwood floorboards covered with a thin layer of earth formed the "natiq," the image of the "nuna"—the land itself. The house's domed roof was the image of the sky, and called by the same name, "qilak." Although there were only two of them, the grandmother and grandson occupied their own little universe.

In those days, everyone had to find their own food, and the grandmother and grandson were running out. The People had a sort of treaty relationship with the Animals. Because the Animals were fast, human hunters could not catch them. Because they were strong, human hunters could not overpower them. Because they were wise, humans could never outsmart them. Therefore, hunters could catch only those Animals who would offer themselves, sacrifice themselves, to provide food and clothing to the otherwise helpless Human Beings. And the Animals gave themselves only to People who expressed their gratitude, treated them with respect, and approached them with humility.

One day, the "maurluq" (grandmother) said to her "tutgarluq" (grandson), "It is time for you to begin to hunt. I have prepared all your weapons and tools. I have decorated them as beautifully as I can, so the Animals will see our care, our respect, our desire to *please them and treat them well. We must count on their willingness to offer themselves to you, or we will soon starve. Walk out across the tundra quietly, respectfully, and watch carefully. Whatever animal gives itself to you, bring it directly home and that will be our supper."*

The boy was happy to have permission to go out on his first solo hunt and he felt a certain pride in being given this responsibility. He only hoped the Animals would cooperate.

Early that morning he began his hunt across the soft, pillowy tundra. After stumbling over its uneven surface for hours, he sat down in frustration on a piece of driftwood near the bank of a slough. The Animals were not coming to him. He had spotted no prey all day and needed to rest. Just as he stretched out his "kameksiik" (skin boots) in front of him, a tiny shrew scampered across his foot.

"Where did it go?" he shouted, as he grabbed a nearby stick. The little mouse reemerged from its hole and the boy whacked it instantly. Holding it in his hand he recalled his grandmother's instructions, "Whatever you catch, bring it directly home and that will be our meal."

"Humm…" he groaned. "We'll have mouse soup for supper tonight. It will be very watery. There will hardly be any meat in that pot. Maurluq will get about half a bite, I will get the other half, and long before morning, we will both be very hungry again. Then I will have to hike all the way out here again in search of food. By that time I will be exhausted and starving. This shrew is too tiny to take home to Grandma. She might even laugh at me if this is all I have to show for my first day's hunting. I might as well make that soup right here and eat this myself. I need to keep up my strength. If I do, I will be able to continue my search, and find something better for Maurluq."

Rationalizing his behavior in this way, the grandson built a little fire, brought the water to boil, and quickly created his mouse soup meal. He then continued on with his hunt.

At sundown, he reached a pond in which there were dozens of muskrat. Using his bow and arrow, he shot one who had approached him while the others swam away. Now he had enough meat for one person's dinner. As he looked at the muskrat, he began to think.

"If I take this home to my grandmother, we will have to share it, so what would have satisfied one of us will not be enough for two. I am so hungry. This muskrat is too small to take home to Grandma. She might even laugh at me if this is all I have to show for my first day's hunting. I may as well roast it here and eat it myself. I need to keep up my strength. If I do, I will be able to continue my search and find something better for Maurluq."

He convinced himself to eat that muskrat and remain overnight on the "nunapik" (the Real Land), the tundra. After enjoying his muskrat meal, he fell quickly to sleep.

The next morning, the boy resumed his hunt and by midday came to a large lake in which there was a colony of beavers. Most of them swam away from him, but one came closer. Once it was within range, he speared it. Now a beaver is much larger than a muskrat, usually enough to feed ten people or more, but the boy had not really had a full meal in two days and he was again getting very hungry. Without even thinking about his grandmother, he ate the whole beaver, stretching his belly beyond its normal capacity.

He continued his hunt, moving toward the shore of the Imarpik, the Bering Sea. There he soon killed a seal, weighing a hundred pounds, and ate the whole seal. Then he killed a sea lion, weighing almost a ton, and ate the whole sea lion. Then he killed a walrus, weighing several tons, and he ate the whole walrus. Then he found a freshly beached whale and ate the whole whale. And, finally, he was so thirsty, he swallowed the ocean.

By this time, all his eating had stretched and reshaped the boy into a giant—tall, wide, and ugly. He began his trek homeward slowly, lumbering along like a huge monster, his heavy feet shaking the ground with each ponderous step. The thunderous sound of his approach alerted Maurluq of his coming long before he arrived at their house. The boy had become so big, fat, and ugly that his home looked tiny to him. He towered over it as the giant he had become, and began to cry.

His grandmother called out to him rather innocently, "Tutgaurluuq, is that you out there?"

Tearfully he replied, "Yes, Grandma, it's me!"

"Well," she said, "Come in, Dear."

"I can't!" he wailed.

"Well, why not, Dear?"

"I brought home too much food!" he replied.

After a moment of thoughtful silence, Maurluq proposed a solution.

"Climb up on the roof, then," she instructed.

The boy was afraid to obey. The house was so little, his feet so big, his body so heavy. If he stepped on that "qilak" it might collapse, destroying the house and crushing his grandmother. But he was even more afraid to disobey his grandmother again.

He carefully put his huge feet on the roof and, mercifully, it did not cave in. "Okay," he shouted to Maurluq. "I'm on the roof!"

"Now jump in, through the smoke hole!" she commanded.

The smoke hole, in the middle of the roof, looked so tiny. He wondered how it would be possible for him to reenter the house through such a miniscule opening, but he somehow had confidence that his elder knew what to do. Trusting in her wisdom, he threw himself up into the air, and fell rapidly toward the opening.

Grandmother held up her magical ivory sewing needle and he passed through the eye of that needle into the house. He was restored to his normal size and all the food he had brought home burst forth, the ocean, the whale, the walrus, the sea lion, the seal, the beaver, the muskrat, and even that tiny shrew.

"Oh, my Grandson!" Maurluq exclaimed in delight, "What a good provider you are!"

NOTES

I first heard this story at the home of one of the most gifted storytellers I have ever met, Maggie Lind, who at that time resided in Bethel, Alaska. She used to walk each day to the local public radio station, KYUK, and tell Yup'ik stories in both Yup'ik and English. Having been raised in the Moravian Children's Home near Kwethluk, she was familiar with European folk tales and bedtime stories as well as the traditional legends of her own people. When she ended this story in Yup'ik she turned to me and said, "Now I want to tell it the 'Kass'aaq way." And she retold it in English exactly as she had told it the first time in Yup'ik. But she changed how the story ended:

"You know," she said, "in that ocean was a ship. And aboard that ship was a very handsome sea captain. And grandma fell in love with him, and they got married and they sailed away and lived happily every after!"

(A Hollywood ending for her 'Kass'aaq audience.)

The traditional version of this story has been told for many centuries, and like the legends of many hunting people, it depicts a boy who disregards an elder's guidance and gets himself into a dangerous predicament. Only the wisdom and power of his grandmother can restore him to his normal size and allow him to return to the life he has lost.

Through his acts, the grandson becomes something inhuman, unnatural. He has left his own world and entered another reality. He cannot reenter his home through the normal passage, the way he exited, but has to be brought back into his world through the smoke hole, the passage from another world back into this one.

Children must be taught how to become Human Beings. If they are not taught, or if they reject the wisdom of the elders, they may not become adults, Real People. They can fail to grow up and remain as children, turning into creatures that no one would want to have in the house.

When I discuss this story with teenagers in rural Alaska today, I ask them for their interpretation. They all have heard this story when they were younger, a story that has been told and retold for generations in southwestern Alaska. All these discussions focus first on the boy's selfishness. He cares only for himself. He forgets all about his starving grandmother. This is the most obvious flaw in the boy's behavior. He is behaving like a child — for infants, toddlers, and children care only about themselves. What I want, what I like, what makes me happy, what gives me comfort, what provides me with amusement — these are the only focus of a baby's life. The slightest irritation or deprivation and they cry! We are all born like this, and behave like this when we are infants.

Growing up and becoming a Real Human Being requires us all to adjust our behavior to accommodate the needs of others. We cannot always have things our way. The boy became a successful hunter, but he hunted only for himself. The Animals do not give themselves to the hunter to feed him only. They offer themselves to him so that he might provide for his family, his neighbors, his community. Keeping all the food and consuming it himself transforms this boy into an alien creature, a monster no one would recognize as human, a giant who does not fit into the house anymore, and cannot live among Real People.

Growing up in some cultures is considered to be almost an automatic process. Teenagers get a driver's license, then a high school diploma, eventually turn 21 and are considered to be adults.

The wisdom of the Yup'ik culture tells us that growing up is a matter of choice. A teen must decide to grow up, become an adult—behave like a Human Being. Children become members of society by realizing that the purpose of their existence goes beyond satisfaction of their own selfish desires, whims, or passions. Each must become the servant of something other than, and more important than, his or her self.

Boys are challenged to reorient the focus of their lives as they gain hunting skills. When a boy catches his first duck, his first muskrat, his first beaver, his first seal, the family will celebrate his achievement with a feast. Friends, relatives and neighbors will attend, perhaps even bringing small gifts. The meat itself is given away. He eats none of it. He does not hunt for himself. The Animals do not give themselves to him alone, but through him, to the community. By hunting he becomes the servant of his family, friends, neighbors, his relatives. If a boy does not undergo this voluntary transformation and cannot turn himself into an adult, he may remain forever a boy, caring exclusively for and focusing totally on himself. In modern society, there are many 30-, 40-, 50-year-old boys.

The story has other possible meanings. The boy ate everything he caught, and with each new catch he was stretched, grew, and changed gradually into a creature he did not intend to become. From a modern perspective, we can take this as fair warning from the First People not to consume things that can change us for the worse, such as drugs, alcohol, and junk food—all of which contribute to major social and health problems in modern society. The wisdom contained in these old legends continues to challenge and inform those who are willing to receive it.

THE FATE OF FATHER JUVENALY

A STORY FROM YUP'IK HISTORY

In 1794, the first group of Christian missionaries to work in Alaska arrived on Kodiak, having walked and sailed over 8,000 miles from Lake Ladoga, on the Russian border with Finland. One of the priests in this delegation of ten monks, a 35-year-old former military officer, Father Juvenaly, was assigned the task of visiting and preaching among the tribes of the southcentral mainland. He began at Kenai, headed northward through what is now the area surrounding Anchorage, then down the western coast of Cook Inlet, across to Lake Iliamna, and out to the Bering Sea.

His journey would bring him from the biggest lake in Europe to the biggest lake in Alaska. But soon after he departed for Iliamna, he disappeared. No one ever heard from him again. Rumors reached Kodiak that he had been murdered, but there were no eyewitnesses or any other conclusive evidence of his whereabouts for several decades.

Then, about a hundred years later, an American historian, Hubert Bancroft, published an account of Father Juvenaly's death purportedly based on the priest's own words as he recorded them in a diary that a man named Ivan Petrov claimed to have found and translated. According to this diary, Father Juvenaly fell into temptation, having been seduced by the daughter of a local Indian chief, and then was hacked to death for refusing to marry her.

That is all I knew about this incident until my Yup'ik father-in-law, Adam Andrew, who was born about 1914 in the mountains near the source of the Kwethluk River, decided to tell me the story about "the first priest to come into our region."

According to my father-in-law, this first missionary arrived at the mouth of the Kuskokwim, near the village of Quinhagak, in an "angyacuar," a little boat. He approached a hunting party led by a local angalkuq (shaman) who tried to dissuade the stranger from coming any closer to shore. The Yup'ik tried to signal their unwillingness to receive the intruders, but the boat kept coming. Finally the angalkuq ordered the men to prepare their arrows and aim them threateningly at the priest. When he continued to paddle closer, the shaman gave the order and the priest was killed in a hail of arrows. He fell lifeless to the bottom of the boat. His helper (in Yup'ik, "naaqista," literally "reader"—someone who supposedly assisted the priest at services) tried to escape by swimming away.

Jumping overboard, he impressed the Yup'ik with his ability to swim so well, especially under water. They jumped into their kayaks and chased the helper, apparently killing the poor man, reporting later that this was more fun than a seal hunt.

Back on shore, the shaman removed the brass pectoral cross from the priest's body and tried to use it in some sort of shamanistic rite. Nothing he tried seemed to work satisfactorily. Instead of achieving its intended effect, each spell he conjured up caused him to be lifted off the ground. This happened several times until finally, in frustration, the shaman removed the cross and tossed it to a bystander, complaining that he did not understand the power of this object, but he no longer wanted to deal with it.

When I first heard this version of the story, I was dubious that such an incident could have occurred. I knew the first priest to come to the Kuskokwim had arrived in 1842, had served on the Yukon for nearly 20 years, and had died in retirement at Sitka in 1862. It did not occur to me that this was the oral account of the death of Father Juvenaly, until I later learned that the Bancroft/Petrov report was completely false—a fabrication of Mr. Petrov's rather fertile imagination.

Hubert Bancroft, the preeminent American historian of his time, never came to Alaska and did not know Russian, the language in which all the earliest historical documents relating to Alaska were written. He hired Petrov to gather documents and translate them, but Petrov did not like Mr. Bancroft much and falsified a lot of data, creating entire chapters of what became the first history of Alaska from records that never existed.

Father Juvenaly's diary was one of Petrov's concoctions. This becomes obvious as soon as any informed scholar opens the manuscript, still housed in the Bancroft Library at the University of California, Berkeley. Juvenaly travels on ships that never existed, celebrates church holidays on the wrong dates and even the wrong months, and miraculously understands Yup'ik within a few weeks, while finding Kodiak's Alutiiq language beyond his reach. These two languages are so closely related that speakers of one believe they can readily understand speakers of the other. Not knowing enough about Russian Orthodoxy to spot glaring discrepancies, Bancroft accepted the diary as authentic, and used it as the basis of his chapter on the death of Father Juvenaly.

Once I realized the published accounts were bogus, I went back to my father-in-law for another telling of the Yup'ik version. We then started to hunt for corroborating evidence. I found that every visitor to Quinhagak in the 70 years following Father Juvenaly's demise mentioned in their reports that this was the site of the incident. I heard from people in the Iliamna area that their ancestors knew nothing of a priest being killed in their region, but only that one had passed through, heading west. I heard from the Cook Inlet Tanai'na Indians that a priest who had come from Russia via Kodiak had baptized them, then left heading in the direction of Iliamna. And I discovered that the people in the village of Tyonek have always had a great swimming tradition, and are still capable of diving into the ocean after the beluga whales they hunt. The oral accounts among all the Native peoples of the region were consistent with my father-in-law's story. But how to prove it accurate, one way or another?

Finally, another scholar discovered a passage in the diary of a later missionary resident of Quinhagak, Rev. John Kilbuck, written sometime between 1886 and 1900, indicating that the first white man killed in the region was a priest who had come upon a hunting party camped near the beach. After trying to dissuade the priest from approaching, and unable to turn him back, the hunting party killed him. His companion tried to swim away "like a seal" and was hunted by the Yup'ik, who had to resort to their kayaks to chase him. The same story that my father-in-law had told me was being told in the village a century after the actual incident.

I have friends who visit and students who reside in Quinhagak, as well as a nephew who lives there. I asked them if they had ever heard the story of how the first priest to visit there was killed. I discovered that the story is still known and told almost verbatim the way my father-in-law told it to me.

Contrary to popular misperception, the oral tradition of tribal peoples tends to be very accurate, for the most part ensuring that stories remain intact over time. The story is understood as community property, not the invention of the storyteller, and, unlike my eastern European family's tendency to change a story to make a point, in groups whose histories are transmitted through the oral tradition, retellings tend to be more faithful to the original story.

However, after looking at my written summary of the story of Father Juvenaly as it had been told to me, one informant did tell me that in a version of the story he had heard, there was a detail I had not been told. According to the story as it had been given to him, just before the priest's death, while standing up in his little boat, he appeared to those on the shore to be trying to swat away flies. At first, this seemed to me a strange detail to include. What did it mean? What was really happening? When someone is about to die, facing his attackers with their arrows pointed at him, why worry about insects?

Puzzled by this account, I kept returning to this scene in my mind until it occurred to me what may have been going on. The man in the angyacuar could have been either praying, making the sign of the cross upon himself, or blessing those who were about to kill him—but so rapidly that to those on shore who had never seen anyone do this, it could well have looked like he was "chasing away flies." This detail from the oral tradition is a perfectly believable addition to the story, and adds credibility to the story itself, as Quinhagak people remember it.

After carefully looking at everything I could find on this incident, I sent a summary of my research to one of my university students from Quinhagak and asked her what she made of the incident. She replied, somewhat sheepishly, "Well, they didn't know he was a priest!"

The question remained, though, why were these armed men so fearful of an unarmed stranger, whom they so vastly outnumbered? True, he was pale, tall, bearded, and oddly dressed. He likely appeared exotic, if not totally alien. But why would they have felt so threatened by his physical presence as to destroy him?

The answer may reside in the brass cross he wore. We know from exhibits at the Smithsonian Institution in Washington, D.C., that at that time shamans carved ivory chains in imitation of their counterparts on the Siberian coast, who wore metal chains. Wearing such a metal chain was an indication that the stranger had spiritual powers possibly superior to the local angalkuq. The only way to defend oneself from such alien magic would have been to kill the magician. So it seems Father Juvenaly died in a case of mistaken identity.

This history lesson tells us that while historical texts may contain many useful details and important data, they can be wrong. Historians usually must depend on what is left behind in the reports, diaries and letters of others, in order to piece together a description of another time and place, and it is easy to be misled, mistaken or fooled. Such was the case with the death of Father Juvenaly two hundred years ago. It has taken nearly two centuries to solve the mystery of his disappearance and death. Original published accounts were based on false and forged information, but the truth survived in the oral tradition of the Yup'ik people.

At least when dealing with the Native experience in this land, no one should dismiss the stories as the indigenous peoples tell them. In my experience, while the published texts have often proven unreliable, grandpa has always been right.

THE TLINGIT WORLD

Preceding page: The Tongass Tribe dances during the First Annual Conference of Tlingit Clans and Tribes, Haines-Klukwan, May 1993.

Top: Clan elders of Angoon and a display of at.óow during a ḵoo.éex' in 1985.

Bottom: A subsistence harvest of sockeye salmon at Little Basket Bay in 2002.

Photos by Peter Metcalfe

BALANCE AND RECIPROCITY

The Tlingit* world is as different from the Yup'ik as could be. The Yupiit live on flat, frozen tundra—big sky country, carpeted with tiny plants, lichens, berries, and grasses. The Tlingit live in one of the few remaining temperate rainforests on earth. The Yup'ik world is treeless; the Tlingit world is covered by trees. The Yup'ik world is flatter than Kansas; the Tlingit world is more mountainous than Wyoming. The Tlingit travel protected ocean waterways that rarely freeze; the Yup'ik are surrounded by an ocean of tundra that is difficult to traverse unless frozen.

According to their own stories, preserved and passed down through generations under the rules of oral tradition, the Tlingit migrated during the last ice age to the coastal area that is now Southeast Alaska. Here they adapted well to the relatively mild, wet climate, and thrived in one of the world's richest ecosystems. They built wooden homes, carved wooden canoes, and erected ornate, totemic house posts, all the while designing intricately carved bowls, ladles, spoons, paddles, masks, rattles and even armor from the spruce and cedar wonderland that is their homeland—"Tlingit Aaní," "the Land of the Tlingit," "the Land of the People."

---

*Many non-Tlingit tend to pronounce the tribal name, which means The People, as "KLING-kit." It is impossible to spell the word phonetically in English, but a more appropriate spelling would be Lingit, pronounced something like "LING-git." The "L" in Tlingit is pronounced by placing the tongue in the position of an English "L," but the sound is produced in the throat. One uses the larynx to actually say "L." In Tlingit, the "L" is always voiceless, meaning that while arching the tongue and touching the back of the teeth, the sound itself is made by forcing air along and then out the sides of the tongue. This is the sound with which Tlingit begins.

The Tlingit collectively represent the second largest tribe of Native Americans in the United States.

Tlingit society is organized into two major social groups, known as "moieties," composed of complementary clans. A member of one clan had to marry someone from a clan of the opposite moiety. Ravens marry Eagles, Eagles marry Ravens.

To use a sports metaphor, the moieties are somewhat like the American and National leagues—ask baseball fans which team they support, and no one who knows what he is talking about says, "My favorite team is the National League!" Tlingits are born into a clan that is either of the Raven or the Eagle moiety, and like any team player his or her allegiance is to the team (clan), while the team's affiliation with the league (moiety) is unquestioned—that is just the way it is.

In the modern era, the symbol of the Raven and Eagle together has become the coat of arms, the "logo," for the entire Tlingit nation.

Tlingit social structure is based on balance and reciprocity. To this day, ceremonial events do not occur—would be meaningless—without the attendance of the opposite moiety. Traditionally, ceremonial events always resulted in the payment or accrual of debts—which could range from gifts or honors of great value to what we might call "favors owed"—an exchange often so subtle and tacit that an outside observer could hardly notice. Contributions of one side—the singing of a song, recognition or praise—all required a response from the opposite moiety.

In traditional times, a village was composed of a collection of clan houses, each of which was decorated with the heraldry of the clan, the way a castle in Europe would bear the insignia of the titled family that owned it. The front of a Tlingit longhouse would be richly decorated with the clan crest. [There is no evidence that totem poles existed in Tlingit Aaní previous to the Euro-American contact era. These were likely the result of a cultural exchange with southern neighbors such as the Tsimshian and Haida that occurred coincidental to contact.] A Tlingit newly arrived at a strange village could find his relatives simply by looking for the house that displayed his coat of arms. It would be as if the Pennsylvanians always hung a replica of the Liberty Bell in front of their house, the New Yorkers a replica of the Statue of Liberty, the Georgians a Peach, the Texans a Lone Star, and the Alaskans, stars depicting the Big Dipper. Everyone in the Tlingit nation knows and recognizes the insignia of each clan. Entering the house of one's own clan, a visitor would identify himself by his name, clan, house of origin, and lineage.

For example, my own Tlingit name is Ku̲xwoosgáa̲x. Loosely translated it means "Call Back" and refers to the echo of a wolf's cry. The name relates to a common wolf behavior, and therefore indicates some connection to the wolf, the insignia of the Kaagwaantaan clan. Now, Kaagwaantaan does not mean wolf. G̲ooch is the Tlingit name for wolf. But members of this clan are often called members of the "wolf clan," because their crest is the wolf. This is not unlike the way sportscasters refer to the college or professional teams whose play they are describing. One can say "the Huskies" just scored again, or one can say "the University of Washington," or simply "Washington" just scored. "The Forty-Niners" just fumbled the ball, can also be expressed as "San Francisco" just lost the ball. The official name of the team and its logo are used interchangeably, and everyone who is familiar with the team and the way the game is played has no problem understanding this. In a similar fashion, each clan is identified with its totem, its at.óow (ut-OO: "ut" rhymes with "cut").

The concept of at.óow is fundamental to the Tlingit way of seeing the world, the Tlingit way of understanding and playing the game of life. At.óow is technically "something owned." And everything of any importance or significance in Tlingit culture is owned. This is enforced even in the way the Tlingit language operates grammatically. For example, when trying to translate the invocation of the Christian God into Tlingit, it is grammatically impossible to say "the Father, the Son and the Holy Spirit." In Tlingit this must be rendered "Our Father, His Son and Their Holy Spirit," all expressed with a possessive modifier. In the Tlingit world it often seems as if everything is owned.

"Some things," one might say, "are more owned than others." Clans have regalia and ceremonial costumes that have been handed down for generations. These embody the clan's crest, and are displayed only on rare, special occasions—primarily at a k̲oo.éex' (koo-EEKH), a memorial, or literally invitational, feast that is usually held about a year after a Tlingit has died.

Like vestments that are worn only when a religious rite is being performed, but never used for any other purpose, the blankets, robes, tunics and head-dresses of the clan are kept in elaborately carved bentwood boxes and brought out only on appropriate occasions. Someone in the clan inherits the responsibility to serve as custodian for the at.óow, but, like the reigning ruler in a monarchy, the "owner" of the at.óow does not literally possess the objects as personal property. The Queen of England may own ten limousines, five palaces, and a thousand evening gowns, and what she does with these is of no national importance. She also owns the crown jewels, the scepter, the orb, and the crown itself, covered in fantastic and historically significant gems. These types of objects are a different story. If Queen Elizabeth were to sell or pawn the Crown, there would be a nationwide uproar. In this sense, these objects are British at.óow.

All Tlingit names are at.óow. Children receive a name at birth, and may receive other names throughout their lives, comparable in some ways to the situation of an heir to the throne in a monarchy. Prince Charles has been the Prince of Wales for many years. His real name should be Charles III, King of the United Kingdom of England, Scotland, Wales and Northern Ireland. He does not have this real name yet, because he has not yet been crowned king. He cannot become king until the throne is vacated when his mother retires, abdicates or dies. Until she does, Charles cannot yet call himself by the name that is his birthright. This is the situation similar to those Tlingits who by birthright or through acquired status become heirs to names, names that have passed down from previous generations and link the individual to the clan and its history. This will occur at a koo.éex', which is both a memorial for the person who has died, and often a "coronation" for the successor who may receive the Tlingit name of the deceased, and usually custody of the regalia—the clan's "crown jewels."

In the Tlingit culture, at.óow are owned by the clan, and responsibility for the "crown jewels" generally resides with the caretaker, the head person of the clan. When the caretaker dies another ascends to leadership of the clan and becomes the caretaker of the at.óow. Then he or she will die, and the process will repeat.

In pre-contact times, two clans trying to solidify their relationship would sometimes arrange marriages. A Tlingit well-educated in the culture would know the clan membership of other Tlingits and their approximate social rank. The aristocracy within each clan can be readily identified by name alone, and marrying below one's social rank was, and sometimes still is, considered undesirable. In this sense, Tlingit society mirrored that of medieval Europe when families of nobles arranged marriages to solidify their social standing, resolve debts or gain allies.

After two Tlingits married, they usually resided with the husband's clan. A matrilineal society, the children would be members of their mother's clan, but Tlingits were also very much patriarchal in the sense that men traditionally "stood up" for the clan. Recognizing the deep affection parents held for their children, long ago it became the responsibility of the mother's brothers to train her sons. It was believed that fathers would be too lenient, but uncles had no such qualms. The boys would be sent to live with their uncles, who were as strict as necessary, even brutal, in order to properly train their nephews in the beliefs, protocols, prohibitions and responsibilities of being an adult male member of the clan. The uncles made men of their nephews.

Notice, then, what would be happening in a kind of weaving pattern across any traditional Tlingit community. The daughters of one generation would be leaving their home for their husband's house, but within a decade her sons would be returning there to be raised by their uncles. It is a kind of inter-family population exchange. Because of this interweaving, Tlingits speak with great fondness of their "in-laws." In the old days, some of the worst and longest-lasting feuds were between clans of the same moiety—the links between Raven clans, for instance, were much more tenuous than the marriage-knit Raven and Eagle clans.

The familial ties are further strengthened during important life events. When Tlingits die, their own family and clan go into mourning and members of the opposite moiety provide all the needs for the funeral. They perform the burial and feed all the mourners who come from other towns. Then, forty days after the funeral, the clan of the deceased hosts a "Forty Day Party," at which they thank and compensate their in-laws for their support and kindness during their bereavement.

The modern non-Native world provides little opportunity for dealing with loss and grief, most often expecting those who have lost a loved one to return to their jobs and resume their normal activities within a few short days. Tlingit may recognize that the modern world has brought them many benefits, but they also recognize that their traditional way of dealing with loss and grief is far more Human. In the face of death, the Tlingits come together in complementary roles, providing comfort and support for each other, acting to restore harmony to lives thrown off balance by the passing of a loved one.

Usually about a year after the funeral, the clan of the deceased invites all the clans of the opposite moiety to an elaborate feast, a koo.éex'—or "pay-off party," in memory of the deceased and in honor of the living who share the same names. These guests from the opposite side will be fed, entertained and given gifts in memory of the one who has died and in honor of the living—"in the name of" them both. The prestige of one's clan will be measured by how well it can conduct, and especially how much it can give away, at their koo.éex'. But one should not infer from this that the potlatch, as it is often called in English, is essentially or even primarily an economic competition, as some anthropological researchers have inferred. The koo.éex' is a deeply spiritual event. At its heart is a determination to honor the ancestors, the departed, and to console those who have lost a beloved, respected elder—as well as to pass on to the next generation the stories, the regalia, the dances and the names which are their birthright.

To this day, koo.éex' remains a central and vital element of Tlingit life. The amount of food served, the length of speeches given, dances performed, and gifts distributed has increased in the last century. The last time I attended a koo.éex', in a village of about 800 people, over $100,000 in gifts of cash and appliances, blankets, clothing and household goods were distributed to the honored guests of the opposite moiety. Each koo.éex' feels like a once-in-a-lifetime event.

An Angoon ḵoo.éex' in 1985. *Photo by Peter Metcalfe.*

Any koo.éex' begins with formal speeches "For the Removal of Grief." Honored members of opposite clans are invited to prepare and deliver speeches to comfort their in-laws and bring the mourning period to a close. Often beautiful, always highly metaphorical, some of these formal speeches in Tlingit rise to the level of or exceed the complexity of the finest Shakespearean oratory.[*]

The very structure of Tlingit presentations can, however, become a stumbling block for those trying to comprehend and appreciate them. The "rules of the game" of Tlingit storytelling differ greatly from the rules by which European orators play. The internal logic of a Tlingit speech is often circular, while European speeches are almost always linear—following the structure many of us learned to outline in school: Roman numeral I then capital A, B, C, then Arabic numbers 1, 2, 3, and for minor details, lower case letters, a, b, c. People schooled in one structure may have difficulty communicating with those who employ the other.

I had this experience after living a few years in Sitka, in the heart of Tlingit Aaní. There was a well-respected aristocratic man who was considered one of the finest and most eloquent of his generation, a man who seldom spoke to me during my two-year residence in his city. I had tried to learn more about Tlingit language by enrolling in a class at a local college, but the instructor focused much more on his own biography and experiences than on such things as vocabulary. We learned to say precious little in Tlingit during that term.

The following summer I flew off to the Yup'ik region where I found myself immersed in the language and culture of Southwest Alaska. I did not return to Sitka for several years, but soon after I did, this same respected aristocrat invited me to his home for dinner. Highly honored, I enthusiastically accepted.

We ate in the relative silence of a traditional supper. Most Alaskan Natives consume their meals carefully, paying close attention to their food, keeping conversation to a minimum. There

---

[*] See the collection of such speeches compiled, transcribed, translated and published under the title *Haa Tuwunagu Yis: For Healing Our Spirit*, by Richard and Nora Dauenhauer. This volume is a testimony to classic Tlingit culture and oratory.

are legends in many cultures about boisterous and inattentive children at the table accidentally spilling or ruining their food, and in the process offending the Animals, who then withhold themselves from the Human Beings that year. A singular act of carelessness can invite disaster. Better to sit and eat quietly, and chat later.

As dessert was served, my host began a traditional Tlingit legend. He obviously enjoyed telling the story, which he related with great detail and enthusiasm. When he finished, I mistakenly assumed that, in order to preserve balance, it was my turn to tell a story, to reciprocate with some yarn of equal color and imagery, but my host interrupted me. No, he had more to say. And he launched into another story, more complex and rich than the first. He no sooner completed that story when he began a third. When he had completed his final story, I was dismissed, by then well aware of the message he had delivered.

During the preceding years, this elder apparently had noted my interest and growing competence in Yup'ik with some alarm. I had been adopted into his nation too, after all. So he had invited me to his home to deliver a focused message that wove three traditional Tlingit legends together, forming, as best I can describe it, an arch in the air with each one, then attaching them in sequence, one after the other, until ultimately he constructed a complete circle. He wove these three stories completely around the central point he was trying to make, and then I was dismissed. His purpose and point were made obvious, even though he never explicitly stated them.

I found the experience to be absolutely amazing. How did he do that? I couldn't do that! How do you edit and shape your stories in such a way as to make an important point to an unsuspecting listener, without ever saying it outright? How do you talk around something with confidence and remain certain that you have communicated what you intended to convey?

He built his circle, segment by segment, then awaited my reaction. Once he saw his storytelling had succeeded, his mission was accomplished. The point around which he so persuasively spoke was this: "Since we Tlingit are so fascinating, why are you so involved with those Eskimos?" But, of course, he never actually said that at all!

In the Tlingit world, names, art, songs, dances, stories—all are at.óow, as are land, resources, history and heritage. There is a lake, for example, near Haines, Alaska, that the Tlingit named "Chilkoot Lake" at "Sockeye Point." These names are owned by a particular clan who use the Sockeye Salmon as their totemic crest, their logo, their coat of arms. This is not because they value or hold this species of fish above other species, but because Sockeye Salmon became their clan crest after a tragedy that occurred on the shores of this lake, at this particular point along the coast.

It seems two boys were canoeing on this lake when a huge sockeye emerged and deliberately tipped over the boat. The boys tried to swim to shore but the malicious fish pulled them under. The boys drowned. This is a terrible loss and injustice, but how does one "get even" with a salmon? Leaders of another clan, the Kaagwaantaan of Sitka, happened to visit at this time and together the two clans decided that from that day forth, that lake, that shoreline and the surrounding area would belong to the Lukaax̱.ádi Clan, and that their insignia would be the Sockeye Salmon. A Chilkat blanket, or ceremonial robe, depicting a ferocious Sockeye, was then commissioned as testimony to this story and its property implications.

Centuries later, some state biologists began installing various fish counting and fish monitoring devices along the shores of Chilkoot Lake, interfering with Tlingit fishing rights without requesting permission. The Lukaax̱.ádi went to court, and their leader testified that this was Tlingit land, that they had owned this shore for many generations, and offered their Chilkat robe as proof of their traditional title. "When white folks want to change ownership, they go to the bank and change the papers. We have no papers. Our ownership has been recognized in history, and it never changes, not for hundreds of years," the court was told. The Lukaax̱.ádi won the case.

While the concept of at.óow and the celebration of the koo.éex' are among the most fundamental principles of the Tlingit experience of life, these customs are but manifestations of a more profound world view. Anyone even superficially acquainted with

Mike Jackson of Kake carving a totem, 1994. *Photo by Peter Metcalfe*

Tlingit art and culture will observe the overwhelming concern for symmetry and balance. What occurs on one side must be mirrored by what happens on the other. This is a social principle central to Tlingit society that not only guides relationships between the moieties, and individual clans and families, but also characterizes the Tlingit view of their relationship to the non-human world. The sockeye monster took two boys from the clan without any provocation or justification. Granting permanent ownership of the lake and surrounding shore, and awarding the image of the sockeye to the Lukaax̱.ádi, was done to honor the sockeye, not to shame it. The transaction rebalanced the scales of justice.

·KEET·

A TRADITIONAL TLINGIT STORY

(Based on several published and dramatized versions of this story)

Naatsilanéi was a great man, an expert hunter, an accomplished artist, a famous orator, and a respected leader. One day, Naatsilanéi's brothers-in-law took him hunting and decided to leave him marooned at a sea lion rookery.

They went out together in a long canoe, hollowed from a single log, and the brothers-in-law and one of his nephews watched as Naatsilanéi leaped from the boat onto the rocks with the ocean waves surging around him on every side. Slippery and wet as everything was, Naatsilanéi demonstrated his agility and skill, harpooning four huge sea lions, killing the first three instantly and injuring a fourth, which escaped. When Naatsilanéi called to his brothers-in-law to help him load these several tons of meat into the canoe, his nephew began to paddle in his direction. Suddenly the brothers-in-law seized the nephew's oar and turned the canoe toward home over the nephew's objections, leaving Naatsilanéi to die of exposure on that rock pile.

As night began to fall, Naatsilanéi wrapped himself in his blanket and tried to get some rest. Suddenly he heard a voice inviting him to "Come with me." He looked up but saw no one. Dozing off, he heard the voice again. "Come with me!" He jumped up this time in search of the voice, but saw nothing. Once again covering up with the blanket, he heard the voice for the third time. He waited for the fourth time and then leapt to his feet. He was shocked at what he saw. Before him was a giant, a man who had emerged *from the bottom of the sea, a man whose outward appearance in the moonlight seemed at first to resemble a Sea Lion.*

"Where do you want me to go?" Naatsilanéi demanded to know.

"Right here," the Sea Lion Man said. "Come with me to my home, beneath this water."

And that giant picked up the edge of the sea as if it were a piece of cloth, revealing to Naatsilanéi the incredible village of the Sea Lion People, who lived under the water in Clan Houses, in a world that paralleled Tlingit society.

Naatsilanéi stepped off the rocks and walked down into the ocean, but he never felt the cold nor tasted the salt. He drifted to the bottom of the sea without any discomfort. There the sea lions guided him to a clan house in which a man lay dying. The Sea Lion People had sent for Naatsilanéi, hoping he would be able to cure their relative. Naatsilanéi suddenly realized this was the fourth sea lion, the one he had harpooned and lost earlier that day. He located the tip of his spear in the sea lion's body and carefully removed it.

The Sea Lion People were so grateful they asked how they might repay their debt to Naatsilanéi. Able to hear his thoughts, they responded before he spoke, bringing him a huge leather bag. It might have been some sort of container; it might have been made from a sea lion hide or stomach. Guiding him back to the surface, the sea lions put Naatsilanéi inside the bag and threw him back into the sea, warning him that if he were to arrive safely back at his village, he was not to think about where he had been or what he had seen, but to keep his mind on his destination.

"If you think about the past," he was told, "you will return to it. If you want to move in a new direction, you must keep your mind and heart focused on that new destination."

Soon after Naatsilanéi was set adrift in the pouch, he began to get anxious about the direction it was floating. "Maybe I'm floating backward to the Seal Lion rookery," he fretted, and, as he did so, he found himself washed back up on that rock.

Inside his mind he heard the leader of the Sea Lions scolding him. "We told you not to think about this place. Leave the past. Focus on the future!"

So Naatsilanéi thought intensely about home, his wife, his people, his family—and his brothers-in-law. He wanted to see them again too! Before long, he had washed up on the beach just outside of his village. He extracted himself from the container the Sea Lions had provided him and began walking home. It was very late. The sun had set, but the full moon provided enough light for him to find his way. Just outside the village he encountered his wife, who had gone out of the house to weep for him in private. How glad he was to see her! How happy she was to see him!

He began to tell her what had happened, how her own brothers had deserted him and left him to die on those rocks far offshore, and she became angry at them. The more details of this crime he related to her, the angrier Naatsilanéi became as well. Finally he ordered her to fetch his axe and adze, his knives and all his carving tools. He had a new project suddenly in mind. His wife was worried about where this would all end, but said nothing and complied with his request.

Naatsilanéi was remembering how when he had visited the Sea Lion village under the water he had seen an amazing creature— a perfect sea creature whom the Sea Lion People had called the "creature of his dreams." It had a long, sleek body, beautiful flukes, fins, and tail, and rows of sharp, white teeth. They called it "Aaní." Naatsilanéi was determined now to create this creature in wood, to carve it, and perhaps to bring it to life.

First he tried to carve the Kéet from spruce wood, but it had no life in it. Then he tried alder, but it sank. Next he tried red cedar with some hope of success, but that proved inadequate as well. Finally, using yellow cedar he carved a Kéet—Killer Whale—that spontaneously came alive. Enthusiastically, Naatsilanéi carved others through the night, and in the morning he sent them on the mission for which they had been created.

He knew his brothers-in-law would soon be going fishing and he wanted to surprise them. He directed the Kéet to attack their boat, smash it to pieces and devour each of those unfortunate men. Only his own nephew, who had tried to rescue him that day on the Sea Lion Rocks, should, if possible, be spared. All the others would die.

It happened exactly as he had hoped. The Kéet attacked the canoe, capsized it, and, like sharks, tortured and devoured the men, leaving only the nephew to survive and drift back to shore to tell the People about the new monster that had entered their world.

Naatsilanéi had his revenge on those would-be assassins. He had killed them all. But this put the world out of balance, for he had actually killed the men who had only attempted to kill him. Only his own death would bring peace. So Naatsilanéi, the great hunter, carver, artist and provider, walked away from his village, deep into the forest, to perish silently, forever weeping for the pain and suffering he had deliberately inflicted on his own relatives.

NOTES

This story is well known, published in several anthologies a century ago, and most recently retold and published in *Haa Shuká: Our Ancestors, A Tlingit Oral Narrative* collected, transcribed, translated and published by Richard and Nora Dauenhauer. Naa Kahidi theater produced a dramatization of this legend some years ago, and a video tape of that performance is available from Sealaska Heritage Foundation in Juneau.

Naatsilanéi's closest friends should be his wife's brothers, for these are the men who would raise his sons. Thus their betrayal is a terrible crime, disrupting the very fabric of the traditional community. But Naatsilanéi's vengeance for their attempt to kill him goes far overboard. In response to their abandonment, he creates the killer whale to violently destroy them. His overwhelming passion for vengeance tips the scales of justice too far in the other direction, and leaves no avenue open for reconsideration or reconciliation. Consequently, there is no way for Naatsilanéi to return home and resume the life he enjoyed before the story began.

Naatsilanéi's journey to the bottom of the sea follows the initiation pattern of a traditional shaman anywhere in the world. Universally shamans acquire their powers by a ritual or actual death and resuscitation. Each must somehow die, have an out-of-the-body experience, and be revived or resurrected. It is through his journey to the depths of the ocean and his subsequent successful return that Naatsilanéi receives the extraordinary ability to create and give life to "the creature of his dreams."

While no one explicitly states that Naatsilanéi becomes an íxt" (shaman) in the telling of this legend, Naatsilanéi's journey and return constitute a typical shamanic initiation.

Kéet do not ordinarily harm or attack people. The only documented cases of a killer whale killing a human being occurred at Sea World, where the humans have violated protocol by denying freedom to the Killer Whales. Once the agreement has been abrogated, all bets are off.

Descendents of Naatsilanéi use the Killer Whale as their crest. The grave of one of the most prominent leaders of this clan, Jimmy George, Sr., who died at an age past 100 years, is marked by a bronze casting of a traditional Killer Whale, created by Juneau Artist Skip Wallen.

SOME TLINGIT HISTORY

The Tlingit were the first Alaska Native group whose homeland was overrun by newcomers in a very short span of time. Within the space of a few months at the end of the nineteenth century, they became a minority in their ancestral land, overwhelmed by prospectors, gold seekers and those other fortune hunters who stampeded north during the Klondike and later Alaskan Gold Rush years.

Prior to this, the Tlingit had insisted that they were sovereign in their own country. They constituted the majority of the population and saw no reason to submit to the ways of the few European settlers who had moved into their territory. They had successfully resisted Russian expansion into the area, and had not been conquered by any foreign power. They continued to understand and play the game of life as they always had.

In the late 1850s, some Tlingit from the village of Kake headed south in several canoes to trade with other Natives and Europeans near Tacoma, Washington. They set up fish camps along the beach and prepared salmon for the coming winter. Unfortunately at about this same time, some Canadian Indians decided to make a series of forays across the border, burning some barns and pillaging some homesteads. The Navy was ordered to find these raiders and return them to Canada. Mistaking the Tlingits, whose homeland was under nominal Russian rule at the time, for the marauding Canadians, the naval officers sent marines ashore and bombarded the Tlingit camp, killing several women and their chief, who was also an íxt' (shaman). The Tlingits were then forced to board the naval vessel and sail to Vancouver Island, where they were deposited and abandoned. Before winter arrived, they carved some new canoes, paddled home, and plotted their revenge.

Sitting safely in the federal customs house on Whidbey Island, retired Army Colonel Isaac Ebey noted that the Navy had almost certainly captured and punished the wrong Indians. He could not know how this misunderstanding would lead to another that would be much more personally tragic.

The following spring, in 1857, the Kake Tlingit sent a war party of their own to find a high-ranking leader of the clan who had killed their shaman. They traveled from settlement to settlement, looking for an aristocrat from the clan whose at.óow was red, white and blue. Coming ashore on Whidbey Island, they found at last a house at which this same at.óow was displayed. They inquired if the person living there was a high ranking leader of this clan and were told that Captain Ebey was indeed a man of high status. So that night they arrived close to midnight at the Colonel's door, knocked and managed to arouse him from bed. When he opened the door, the Tlingit shot and decapitated him, hurrying back to Alaska with the proof that the death of their leader and shaman had been appropriately avenged.

Although the New York Herald Tribune covered this story in great detail, to this day few people are aware that the Tlingit responsible for the beheading at what is now Ebey's Landing State Park did so in retaliation for the unprovoked attack they suffered in Puget Sound a year earlier.

A similar incident occurred twelve years later, in 1869, when a U.S. Army sentry fired at a Kake trading party departing aboard a canoe from the beach in front of Sitka. One of their party was killed. The sentry had mistaken them for a group of Sitka Tlingits who were under a restraining order by the fort's commander, Col. Jefferson C. Davis, until a dispute was settled. The aggrieved Kake Tlingits, while returning to their village on Kuiu Island, encountered and killed two white prospectors in retaliation. This prompted Davis to send the paddle-wheel steamship, *Saginaw*, on a mission of revenge. By the time the vessel arrived in the vicinity of the bay on northern Kuiu that now bears its name, the several Kake villages in the area were prudently deserted. In all, 29 houses were burned and many canoes destroyed by the *Saginaw's* crew.

Early in the Russian period, Kake villages had also been attacked and burned in retaliation for a Tlingit assault on Old

Sitka. Their clan houses burned to the ground twice within a sixty-year period, it is no surprise that many residents of the, by then, consolidated village of Kake decided, early in the twentieth century, to abandon their Tlingit identity. The village passed ordinances forbidding the use of the Tlingit language and destroyed all their own totem poles. Kake decided that the only way to survive in the modern world was for Indians to pretend they had come on the Mayflower instead of welcoming it.

The village of Angoon was also attacked and burned—in 1882—because of a similar misunderstanding. After an íxt' was killed in a whaling accident while employed by the whaling station at Killisnoo just south of Angoon, the Tlingit demanded restitution from the company. In the past, such reparations had been paid since Tlingit customs still governed relations between the Native population and the small minority of European settlers. But, deciding it was time to impose American rule on the Tlingit, the U.S. Navy, based in nearby Sitka, steamed to Angoon to demand a hundred blankets restitution be paid to the company for the lost time and productivity the incident had cost. When the Tlingit could not meet these demands, the Navy bombed, looted and burned Angoon. It took three years to rebuild the village, and much of the community's irreplaceable at.óow were lost or stolen during this confrontation.

A century later, in October 1982, Angoon hosted a healing ceremony to commemorate the tragic misunderstanding and violence of a hundred years before. A videotape of that day-long ceremony contains some valuable insights into the Tlingit mind, and the way the Tlingit grieved and dealt with the loss of so many lives, especially elders and children who suffered in the years following the destruction. They had lost their homes, and their winter food supplies were destroyed, resulting in the starvation of many people. The U.S. Navy was invited to offer an apology at the commemoration ceremony, but declined. To this day, the people of Angoon call upon the Navy to apologize for the punishment of "a crime we never committed."

Violence and forced relocation characterized the relations between Europeans and Native Americans between 1500 and 1880. By the time Alaska became a U.S. Territory, however, Indian policy had shifted toward assimilation. This brought a new set of problems, the aftermath of which Alaskans continue to struggle with to this day. Trying to adapt to the new circumstances, the Tlingit fought for equality and led the fight for citizenship and for equal access to housing and public accommodations, culminating in the Anti-Discrimination Act of 1945, which prohibited any business from excluding anyone from its premises on the basis of race.

Two leaders in this fight for equal rights were Elizabeth and Roy Peratrovich—she a well educated Tlingit woman, adopted by white missionaries as a child, and he the son of a Serbian gold miner and his Tlingit wife. The Alaska Native Brotherhood and Sisterhood originally lobbied for Native American Citizenship, which was awarded to all tribes in 1924, and then for equal protection and civil rights. During a senate debate on the floor of the territorial Alaska Legislature in February 1945 (14 years before statehood), one senator rose to attack the bill. "Far from being brought closer together, which will result from this bill, the races should be kept further apart. Who are these people, barely out of savagery, who want to associate with us whites with five thousand years of recorded civilization behind us?"

Invited to speak on behalf of the bill, Mrs. Peratrovich stood up in the gallery and delivered a brief but brilliant speech: "I would not have expected that I, who am barely out of savagery, would have to remind gentlemen with five thousand years of recorded civilization behind them of our Bill of Rights." She sat down, the Senate voted, the bill passed and the Governor signed it the next day, February 16. This day is now a State holiday honoring Elizabeth Peratrovich.

❧

THE ATHABASCAN WORLD

Preceding page: Snowshoe race.

Top: Katie John and her granddaughter collect spruce roots, summer 1998.

Bottom: Children at play near a fishwheel in the Yukon River.

Photos by Bill Hess

THE DISTANT TIME OF THE FIRST PEOPLE

The Athabascan Family of Indigenous Nations occupies nearly the entire northwest quadrant of North America, though its most famous members, the Navajo and Apache, migrated many centuries ago to an area to the southwest in what is now known as the United States. The Koyukon, Tanana, Gwich'in and Ahtna tribes have lived in Alaska's interior for several millennia. The Tanai'na, who migrated from the far north, today make up the main Native group living along Cook Inlet and Lake Clark.

A land of extremes, the homeland of Alaska's Athabascans is very cold in winter and often hot in summer, its landscape dotted by lakes and streams, featuring North America's highest peak, Denali, or "The Great One"—the Athabascan name given to it hundreds of years before the arrival of Europeans.

The Athabascans lived in small, scattered, nomadic bands, until quite recently, when they settled into permanent year-round villages. They survive primarily by subsistence hunting, fishing and gathering. Although imported, store-bought goods are now available in every town, low cash incomes and the high price of store-bought groceries in this region requires that each family harvest considerable wild foods in order to make ends meet.

Subsistence hunting and gathering in Interior Alaska is much more than a matter of mere economic necessity. These activities manifest the Athabascan world view, a human way of seeing and relating to the world, and to each other. Everything in the Athabascan world is essentially spiritual; no one can fully understand the culture without grasping this central element. The whole world is alive and sensitive.

Stories from the Distant Time teach each generation the ways in which The People show their respect for the spiritual realities that control all life in the sub-Arctic forests that make up the

Athabascan homeland. Trees and mountains, rivers and ice floes all contain spirits that are easily offended. An Athabascan child's education teaches the importance of relating respectfully not only to the human but also to a natural community whose invisible forces dominate the universe.

Athabascans have had to be flexible to survive for so many years in a harsh, forbidding environment, and as a result are perhaps the most adaptive of Alaska's Traditional Peoples, open to new ideas and technologies and willing to incorporate these into the old ways. Visitors to an Athabascan village may think little of the traditional culture remains—it is easy for traditional practices and beliefs to escape the attention of anyone unfamiliar with the Athabascan way of life. Yet, much remains of their ancient world view, the "game of life as they understand and play it."

A central concept for Koyukon Athabascan people involves "luck." This is not the Lady whose favor Las Vegas or Reno gamblers seek. In Athabascan culture, "luck" is more akin to the Christian concept of Grace, or the Buddhist concept of Karma. It is a sort of sacred, invisible force that can be quantified, increased or lost, depending on the behavior of each individual. One can gain or squander "luck" the way one can win or lose money in a casino. Among the Athabascans, luck increases only when a person knows how to behave appropriately, observing the "hutlaanee"—the code of proper behavior derived from the Stories of the Distant Time.

While modern, globalized society is driven by a future orientation—predicting, planning, seeking the newest, the most up-to-date research, eager for the latest data, the latest fashions, etc.—traditional cultures look to Beginnings. There, in that remote and sacred time, structures and patterns were established to forever govern the universe. The goal of an Athabascan education is to provide members of the next generation with an awareness of those eternal models so that they can live in harmony within long-established parameters, and in conformity with traditional ideals.

The structures and standards that were established "in those days," have been transmitted through the ages in stories about how the world began, how various creatures first appeared, and how the people learned what they now know about the laws that govern the world. These stories are considered sacred, revealing eternal Truths about the Universe and the appropriate place of the Human Being within it.

An Athabascan—a Human Being—knows that words and actions have power that must be used appropriately, channeled along established, appropriate lines. Violations of these boundaries can prove catastrophic for the individual, the community, or even all people. A child takes the form of a true Human Being by adhering to these age-old standards, and by observing traditional guidelines and principles.

Perhaps more than any other Alaskan culture, the Athabascans experience their world in terms of Sacred Time, the Distant Time of the First People, and focus on retaining a meaningful relationship with the ancestors through the repetition of actions, in remembrance of Those Days. Ggadanzitnei, the Koyukon term for both the Distant Time and the stories that speak of it, constitutes the core of the way Athabascan people, the Dene, see the world. It is through the Ggadanzitnei that we too can look along the beam of light that conveys the Athabascan view of the universe.

Athabascan women conversing during a potlatch. *Photos by Bill Hess*

THE SALMON GIRL
AN ATHABASCAN STORY FROM NIKOLAI

*U*ntil very recent times, Athabascan peoples had to travel long distances throughout the year to find food. The cold, windswept interior region of Alaska and northwestern Canada where most Athabascan tribes live requires Human Beings to relocate regularly to hunting and fishing camps where, each in its own season, the fish and game provide enough food to sustain them. Meat harvested in fall must last through the winter. Salmon caught, split, dried and smoked in summer must last until spring. If the resource fails, the people starve.

There was a young girl who was particularly interested in the coming run of King Salmon, the greatest of river fish and the first to arrive each spring. For weeks the family's supply of smoked and dried salmon had been dwindling. Her father had decided to put the family on half rations in an attempt to make the limited supply of fish last until the first Kings arrived. The family had been surviving but going to bed hungry for some weeks already, and the girl was anxious. She wanted to be the first to welcome the salmon home. Every morning she leaped and crawled down the river bank and watched the clear, fast-moving waters flow past her village. Where were the Kings? Would they come today? Would she be able to spot them when they finally arrived?

Day after day she sat by the river, waiting and watching. Finally she thought she saw something—perhaps the dorsal fin, perhaps part of the tail of one of those magnificent salmon. The angle of the light and the reflection of the clouds on the surface of the water, however, made it difficult to see very deeply into the water.

She decided to climb up a nearby birch tree and sit on one of its branches to get a better look.

Sure enough, as she wiggled her way out onto one of the lower branches, the King Salmon came clearly into view. Excited and delighted, the girl slipped off the branch and plunged directly into the cold, clear stream. At first she panicked as her clothes and boots filled with water and the current dragged her under. She tried violently to push herself upward, but the weight of her parka and footwear made it impossible for her to float. Then she relaxed and realized she was breathing comfortably. She was being transformed into a fish.

In the form of King Salmon she journeyed upstream with her new friends and watched as they threw themselves over rocks and obstacles, determined to arrive at their own birthplace where they would lay and fertilize their eggs and then give their bodies to the bears and birds who anticipated their arrival with as much appetite as did the Human Beings.

After their summer salmon feast, the birds would migrate south for the winter, while after their banquet, the bears would retire to their dens to sleep for half the year. All the creatures of this land depended on the Salmon. Without them, none could survive. This Land is Salmon Land, and here were the Kings!

As the winter passed, Salmon Girl observed the eggs hatching into tiny fry and then, with spring breakup, these babies swam with the current downstream toward the sea. She joined them as they journeyed toward the muddy mouth of the river and merged into the shallow, nutrient-rich sea. She met whales and walruses, sea lions and seals, as well as dozens of varieties of fish she had never seen in her inland town. She watched with fascination and awe as the various sea mammals and fish swam and played in the cool ocean spray, many leaping for joy until the ice formed a solid lid over most of the water. Her friends showed her their path to the North Pacific where they matured for another two years, doubling in size every twelve moons.

But all salmon get homesick, and Salmon Girl was no exception. She wanted to see her parents, her village, her relatives and friends again. Having learned the language of the salmon, she could overhear the fish discussing whose nets to enter and whose nets to avoid.

"One thing I cannot tolerate," one of the Salmon Sisters maintained, "is dirty drying poles. People should have the decency to clean their spruce branch drying racks after they use them, or replace them with new poles each year. I for one will not enter the net of a Human Being who has not cleaned the poles on which they expect me to be dried or smoked. Who wants to spend the summer on a dirty pole, covered with the blood and flesh of your own relatives? That's disgusting!"

The other Salmon agreed. Then another spoke up. "Although I have never been caught and have not experienced what being skinned or split open must feel like," she began, "I am sure that clean and sharp knives make the process so much less painful and traumatic. I will never swim into the net or take bait from those who have not sharpened their knives and ulus, or cleaned them. I can't imagine why any Salmon would!"

"And another thing," added a third Salmon. "I think it is a scandal that people waste food as much as they do. They say that food is hard to find, that it is hard to preserve and store, hard to harvest, but they pay so little attention to how much they throw away! Why, they don't even take care that the fish they are drying does not get wet in a sudden downpour. There is really no excuse for fish to be hanging with their red flesh facing the sky and having rain fall and spoil that food. It should always be turned over, with its silvery coat facing upward, so that if it rains, the water will flow off the skin and not dampen or mold the fish. People should be more careful, more respectful. Before I let myself be caught and hung on a drying rack, I want to be sure they know how to treat us respectfully. After all, we're the ones dying to keep them alive!"

The Salmon Girl listened to all that her sisters were saying but said nothing herself. She tried to remember all that they had taught her.

Soon it was time to head back upstream. After several days of exhausting swimming against the current, they approached the girl's home village. She leapt for joy, completely out of the water, to get a good look at her family and friends. How happy she was to see them again, after all these years. Some of her Salmon friends were swimming into her parents' net, because they had already ascertained that these people prepared new drying poles every spring, kept their knives and ulus sharp and clean, and never wasted any of their fish.

The Salmon Girl did not want to become her parents' supper. She wanted to be their daughter again. So she threw herself onto the beach and was immediately transformed back into a Human Being. How amazed her mother and father were! They rushed over to her and exclaimed "We thought you had fallen into the river and drowned! We looked for you for days, but found no trace of you. We had given up all hope of ever seeing you again!"

The Salmon Girl explained that she had indeed fallen into the river but had become a King Salmon almost instantly and had traveled down river to the sea and out into the ocean. She had seen many incredible sea creatures and had returned to her home, as all Salmon People do, in order to give herself to the Human Beings. But when she saw her family there, she knew she had to try to rejoin them. She loved and missed them so much!

She told her parents all that she had learned from the Salmon People, how they avoided the nets of those who were dirty, lazy or careless. She taught all her people to clean or replace their drying poles, to sharpen and clean their knives and ulus, and perhaps most importantly, not to needlessly waste any of their food.

Thanks to the wise advice of the Salmon Girl, the Human Beings learned to live in a humble, respectful and grateful relationship with the Salmon People, who return every spring to offer themselves as food to those who need them and are worthy of this precious gift.

NOTES

Historically, starvation haunted Athabascan societies, since their subsistence resources were more scattered and scarce than in some other regions of the state. Forced by circumstances to move from camp to camp, a family's or a tribe's survival often depended on their ability to find sufficient food at critical junctures of the year. Hunger was a constant threat, and watching for the salmon would have been a major preoccupation when the winter supply of dried or smoked fish began to run out.

Changing into an animal is a common theme in Alaskan legends. Learning from the animals by seeing things from their perspective applies to seeing other human points of view as well. The ability to consider an issue from many viewpoints is highly respected among traditional peoples.

The story provides the basis of Athabascan protocols for dealing appropriately with salmon: keep everything tidy and clean, the tools sharp and washed, and pay close attention to the food as it is drying or smoking, being especially careful not to carelessly waste any of it. This is how one becomes a Real Person and keeps the world in balance.

Athabascan potlatch. *Photo by Bill Hess*

THE SLEEPING LADY

AN ATHABASCAN STORY FROM TYONEK

W hen the earth was new, people were different. They were bigger, stronger and smarter. They understood the language of the animals. They knew how to read the sky, the waves, the rain and snow. They could descend to the spirit worlds beneath the earth and ascend to the spirit worlds beyond this one, through the opening in the dome of the sky into places above it. They built their houses as replicas of the world as they imagined it, and behaved in meaningful, appropriate and respectful ways toward each other and all the creatures with whom they shared the world.

In the beginning times, the world was sunny and warm. All kinds of food grew even as far north as Alaska. There were all sorts of flowers, fruits and edible plants. Fruit grew on trees. Life was comfortable, happy and peaceful. The Dena'ina were People of Peace.

Further north were found other tribes who had not yet adapted to this harmonious and respectful way of life. Constant wars raged among these northern tribes, and along the Pacific coast, where villagers regularly raided and pillaged other settlements, taking prisoners, killing, ransoming or enslaving each other. But along the central coast, the Dena'ina lived in peace.

There, a young girl named Susitna made plans to marry a young man named Nekatla. As their wedding day approached, the couple's families became increasingly eager and happy. This union would bring them all together as relatives, making a very large and prosperous clan in which in-laws would treat each other as brothers and sisters. Peace would embrace a yet larger number of Human Beings, as the union of this couple would bring hundreds more into a loving, supportive circle.

The years of peace and prosperity had made the Dena'ina grow in power, but they did not seek to dominate anyone. They were content to be left in peace, even if their neighbors continued to attack and kill each other.

Just before the wedding day, bands of raiders encroached from the north, burning Dena'ina villages and slaughtering entire families. The messenger who brought this shocking news to the village explained that he had been away hunting for several days and had returned to find his entire household dead. The invaders were moving south and would soon come to this village.

The elders summoned an emergency council and asked everyone to express their position. How should the People of Peace respond? Some young men insisted that the time of Peace had ended, and that the Dena'ina would have to take up arms to defend themselves. Others said that the Human Beings should flee into the forest and let the invaders pass through their country. Conflict should be avoided at all costs. Finally Nekatla spoke. He suggested a bold plan. Why not send a peace delegation to the invaders and offer them gifts?

"If we do not resist them they will have no reason to harm or attack us," the young man suggested. "If we treat them with kindness they might relent, leave us in peace."

Since the Dena'ina had embraced peace as their tribal approach to each other and to their neighbors, the counsel accepted Nekatla's proposal. On the day that should have been his wedding day, he set out northward to meet the invaders and offer them gifts of peace and friendship.

Susitna and her friends were heartbroken that their plans had been completely overthrown by these violent and tragic new circumstances, but they hoped Nekatla's mission would succeed. They were confident there would be a future wedding date and many years of happiness afterwards. The young ladies walked some distance from their village and then busied themselves with picking berries and cutting beach grass for baskets throughout the night as well as all day long. The next day and night the young women sat more quietly and wove grass, picking fewer berries.

The third day and night, Susitna sat even more quietly, but more anxiously, unable to sleep as she worried about the fate of her beloved and the outcome of the courageous exploit he had undertaken. She had very little energy to do any more gathering or sewing, but she could not rest. Susitna sat facing northward for several more days, and eventually several weeks, still anxiously awaiting word from Nekatla. Finally exhausted she lay down and fell asleep.

Only after she had collapsed into deep slumber did news arrive that the invaders had refused all the offerings and massacred all the Dena'ina men who had journeyed northward to negotiate peace. There had been a battle in which the Dena'ina had done well, since they were giant people, much taller and stronger than their enemies, but they had come with few weapons and were unprepared for war. All had perished.

Her friends first attempted to wake Susitna, but then realized that there was no point in trying to arouse her. The news would only bring her tremendous sadness, so she could wait to learn of her finance's tragic death. Let her be, they agreed. So Susitna slept on.

Snow fell, covering her in a shimmering white blanket. She did not stir. Spring came and adorned her with a green robe, and summer clothed her with splashes of brilliant berry colors. In autumn, her quilt became bright with fall hues of red, orange, yellow and rust. And Susitna slept on and on.

Centuries have passed now, and Susitna, the Sleeping Lady, remains asleep. People are much smaller now, so she seems like a giant today, lying on her side facing the modern city of Anchorage. She will awake, they say, when the people of the world live in peace, when war is abolished and no one commits violence against another. And Nekatla will then return as well, and the marriage of the Peace Giants will finally be celebrated by all the nations of the earth.

NOTES

This story seems to be of more recent origins than most of the others. Some elder storytellers in the Cook Inlet area do not recall hearing this story in their youth, but recognize that it has been circulating in the area for the last seventy years and is frequently told in the village of Tyonek. For this reason, we attribute this legend to that community and thank them for it. Thousands of tourists from all over the world are introduced each summer to Mount Susitna as "the Sleeping Lady."

Stories about the world when it was new, inhabited by people who were wiser, stronger and larger than ourselves, giants who lived in a sunny, warm paradise, are fairly widespread in Alaska. The "good old days" were long ago, when the First People encountered and were informed by the Creator of the structures of the world and how to live appropriately in this ecosystem. Each generation tends to forget part of this message, so the situation continues to deteriorate. The further you are from the origins, the more distant you are from the Source, the Sacred, and therefore the powerful time when the world was new and filled with energy. As things age, they wear out. It is true of this world, and of each successive generation of Human Beings as well.

Instead of peace spreading to other tribes and nations, it has been violated repeatedly by injustice, bloodshed, hatred and death. The Sleeping Lady may have to sleep for more centuries before the age of peace, gentleness, love and justice dawns.

Preceding page: Aleut boy.

Top: The late Father Peter Bourdukofsky of Unalaska, with his mother, Mary Bourdukofsky of St. Paul, during a visit to Funter Bay where Aleuts were interned during World War II.

Bottom: Dutch Harbor service.

Photos by Bill Hess

MOVING FREELY BETWEEN CULTURES

The origin of the word "Aleut" is something of a mystery. Many believe this name came into use after the second Bering voyage in 1741, when Siberian fur traders failed to distinguish between the Unangax, who inhabit what is today called the Aleutian Islands—the long archipelago that stretches from the tip of the Alaska Peninsula to Attu—and the traditional enemy of the Unangax, the Sugpiaq, known to the Unangax as "Koniaga." The Sugpiaq live near the northern end of the Alaska Peninsula, on Kodiak Island, at the tip of the Kenai Peninsula, and along the shores of modern day Prince William Sound.

Before the coming of the "promyshlenniki" (Slavic trappers and traders from Siberia), the Sugpiaq and Unangax people shared a common ecosystem, mostly treeless and windswept, from which were harvested plentiful fish and sea mammals. The Aleut crafted tools and objects of bone and stone for utility as well as art, and wove exquisite basketry from native grasses. Driftwood was shaped into intricate headgear, including visors used not only for practical purposes, reducing the glare of sunlight on the surface of the sea, but as ceremonial regalia as well.

These are the people who invented and perfected the kayak, and were so adept at hunting seated in these that the Siberians never tried to imitate them. It was easier, they reasoned, to trade for sea otter pelts harvested by kayaking hunters than to attempt to learn to kayak themselves.

Seals, sea lions, and whales provided ample quantities of meat, but the salmon streams on some islands represented the area's richest natural food resource. Rain gear made from the intestines of sea mammals or even from fish and bird skins kept locals dry during the region's frequent damp, foggy and rainy days. The National Museum of Finland in Helsinki displays seal gut parkas, made in the earliest style as a long hooded shirt. By the early 1800s, these raincoats resemble the capes worn by aristocratic Russian naval officers, complete with high, embroidered collars and sleeves. The technique and materials are all indigenous, but the designs reflect Russian influences—celebrations in gut, feather, thread and bead representing the coming together of two worlds in the Aleutians.

The Unangax and the Sugpiaq speak mutually unintelligible languages, and waged war against each other for centuries. When I came to Kodiak Island in 1970, all the "war stories" I heard from elders involved raids and attacks back and forth between their ancestors and the people of Unalaska and Belkovsky to the west. At the same time they spoke of their wars with these inhabitants of the Aleutian "Chain," these same elders insisted that they, the Sugpiaq, were the true "Aleuts."

Years later, when I had the chance to visit the Aleutian Islands, elders there insisted that they alone were the authentic "Aleuts." I even heard an argument between a young man from the Pribilof Islands, in Unangan territory, who recognized that Sugpiaq was very closely related to Yup'ik, as he dismissed a Kodiak area woman's contention that she was Aleut. "You are the Eskimo Aleuts!" he insisted. The Ouzinkie lady indignantly replied, "No, you are the Japanese Aleuts!" If the name were just being inappropriately and inaccurately applied to both very different languages, why would people be arguing about it so vehemently for two hundred years? Perhaps, I thought, they were both mistaken.

If we classify people by the language they speak, the Unangax and Sugpiat are very different tribes. But language and culture are not always identical. For example, Swiss is a culture, not a language. Visitors crossing the border from France to Geneva might not recognize that they had moved into another country. Someone coming from Germany to Zurich might not realize they had crossed any border at all. And entering Switzerland from the south, an Italian might assume he was still in Italy. But just as the Swiss are participants in a culture, not speakers of a common language, I would come to see that the Aleut were similar.

I was once assigned to visit the Yup'ik speaking villages surrounding the shores of Lake Iliamna, where I encountered a

Yup'ik speaking woman who insisted she was also Aleut. I began, rather foolishly and arrogantly to argue with her.

"Were your ancestors originally from the Chain?" I asked.

"No," she answered. "They were from here."

"Well, were some of them from the Kodiak area, perhaps a few generations ago?"

"No," she emphatically replied. "They were from here."

"If they were not from the Aleutian Islands nor from the Sugpiaq region, you cannot be Aleut!"

"But I AM!" she emphasized.

The question of Aleut identity was becoming more frustratingly vague to me. I wondered why three different groups—Unangax, Sugpiaq, and now even some Yup'iks—would so adamantly insist that they were Aleut, often denying that others had a rightful claim to this name.

And then it struck me: This Yup'ik lady who so emphatically defended her "Aleut" ethnicity had a Slavic surname. Maybe, like the Swiss, those who have called themselves Aleut have a common story, a history along which they see their past, and by which they all claim, with some justification, to be "Aleuts." Maybe grandma actually knows what she is talking about! Perhaps the Elders are right and all the professors, history books and atlases are mistaken.

But, if so, how did it happen that all three of these groups came to accept and later defend their identity as Aleut when the name itself, it seems, came from Siberia? This fact is the first clue.

Contact and intermarriage with adventurers and settlers from Russia weave a common thread throughout the most recent 300 years of the Aleut story. During the Cold War, a four-decade ideological conflict between the capitalist West and the communist East (primarily the Soviet Union, i.e., Russia), Aleuts were often ostracized because of their racial and ethnic connection to Russians, and made to feel ashamed of this chapter in their history. Their Slavic heritage is undeniable, as is obvious by the names listed in the village telephone directories. No other part of Alaska has so many last names ending with -of, off, or -sky. My neighbors in Old Harbor were the Melovedoffs, and the village was also home to the Alexandroffs, Bourdukofskys, Malutins, Ignatins, and

Waspikoffs. Some of the most prominent old families in the region were the Squartsoffs, Chernoffs, Kashevarovs and Lukins, and in the Aleutians, Merculiefs, Philemonofs, Lestenkofs, Gromoffs, Lekanofs and Malavanskys.

Slavic trappers and traders, the promyshlenniki, were the first Caucasians to venture into the wilderness of the Russian Far East, where they set up their trading posts and trap lines. These men were mostly loners, bachelors with little affinity for city life, who struck out independently into the forests to "live off the land." Often, their only human contact was with nomadic local tribes, into which they sometimes married, raising bilingual, bicultural offspring, who often continued the pattern, moving deeper into the wilderness to found their own homesteads. In my research I discovered that this had been the pattern in Siberia for centuries before any citizens of the Tsar's empire ventured across the Bering Straits. America had the "Wild West," while Russia had the "Wild East," and in many respects still does.

History books, such as Bancroft's, characterize the first fifty years of contact along the Aleutian Chain as a continuous bloodbath, a time of pillage and massacre that lasted until Alexander Baranov imposed some semblance of order during his tenure as chief manager of the Russian-American Company. Subsequent history books repeated this version of the first decades of contact, which became ever more sanguinary as new histories were published during the Cold War.

Since the opening of the Soviet Union during the perestroika era, and then the collapse of communism in Russia, scholars have taken a fresh look at the history of the Russian occupation of Alaska. It is now a field of inquiry hotly debated and unsettled. Few would argue the fact that Baranov ruled as a dictatorial governor for 27 pivotal years (1791-1818). Whether he was an enlightened ruler or a brutal oppressor remains in question. Time and again, elders have insisted to me that it was Baranov's autocratic rule that depopulated their island, not conflict with the earlier promyshlenniki.

There had been violent confrontations before Baranov's time, notably the massacre at "Refuge Rock" on Sitkalidak Island (near Kodiak Island) in 1784, but to take this atrocity as an indictment

Walter Dyakanof of Unalaska with his great granddaughter, Leona Dushkin..

Photo by Bill Hess

against the promyshlenniki would be to misread history, for it was Shelikov, a founder of the Russian-American Company, who led the attack. Through Shelikov's influence, the Russian-American Company attained a commercial monopoly in Alaska. Baranov was later employed as the company manager and became, in effect, governor of Alaska.

Within a decade of the massacre, the promyshlenniki and local women were intermarrying frequently. This oral tradition version of Aleut history was further substantiated years later when I discovered that a Russian naval vessel had wintered at Three Saints Bay in 1791, and the chaplain aboard that ship was busy for months, marrying dozens of couples there.

These promyshlenniki eventually penetrated Bristol Bay and ventured up the rivers, founding posts and intermarrying with Native women around Iliamna Lake, as well as on the Yukon delta. One finds Slavic surnames today, for example, far up the river, even beyond the town named "Russian Mission."

A third of the Siberians who intermarried with Aleuts were Kamchadal (Native people from Kamchatka Peninsula). Within a few decades of the post-contact period, many Aleuts had become bilingual. By the time the first resident Russian Orthodox clergy arrived from Irkutsk early in the nineteenth century, they found a large population of "Creoles," children of mixed ancestry, who spoke their mother's indigenous language with their maternal relatives, friends and neighbors, while speaking Russian to their fathers and their fathers' colleagues.

Russian missionaries developed writing systems for the local languages (on Kodiak in 1804, and at Unalaska and Atka in 1824 and 1826), and opened schools for the children.

When I first arrived on Kodiak over 30 years ago, I was told the community had invited me to spend the summer running an "Aleut School." I had no idea what this was! Little by little, I came to realize that they wanted their children to continue this bilingual pattern. When I arranged a concluding program, at which my 200 students could demonstrate what they had learned that summer, and they sang in Alutiiq, Slavonic and English, one of the grandmothers commented to me, "We're all so glad, Michael, that you finally got it right!" The last bilingual teacher in Old Harbor, who conducted what they called "Aleut School," had died a few years earlier, and the village was worried that their bilingual tradition would suffer if no one continued this informal (and unfunded) educational effort. On their own initiative they sought a replacement, and not finding anyone in Alaska who could teach both Alutiiq, as they called their Sugpiaq language then, and Russian, they went further afield, finally contacting a Russian Orthodox seminary in the suburbs of New York. That is how I got to Alaska! I knew nothing of this history, nothing of the story into which I was being invited. I had a lot to learn!

Every household in Old Harbor, near Three Saints Bay where Shelikov founded his settlement in 1784, had stories to tell about the old days, dating back to the Russian era. I heard nothing favorable about Baranov, nor any of his henchmen, and in one village I heard a grandmother scolding a naughty child, "Kuskov will get you if you don't behave!" Later I discovered Ivan Kuskov was the commandant at Fort Ross, on California's Sonoma coast, who had pressed unwilling Sugpiaq hunters into company service, forcing them to kayak south, never to return. He became the Alutiiq "boogey man," and is still remembered as such today.

Every family also had Father Herman stories, many of them recounting miraculous healings, especially following a visit to his grave at Monk's Lagoon, on the eastern end of Spruce Island (just off the north end of Kodiak Island) where he had taken refuge from the hostility and persecution of Baranov and his men. Father Herman had defended the Natives from Baranov's exploitation and abuse, risking his life to write reports to governing authorities back in Russia and finally getting out of harm's way by relocating to a hermitage on the only forested island near that part of Kodiak.

Until arriving in Kodiak I knew nothing of this story. But every home had Father Herman stories to tell. I ordered and read aloud to my classes a biography of St. Herman of Alaska, but they seemed rather bored with my lesson. Then it occurred to me that I was not telling them anything new. They had heard these stories all their lives; their parents, aunts, uncles and grandparents were the oral sources for this rich history now at last preserved in print for future generations. While some Russians had oppressed and enslaved Aleuts, the pious and courageous example of this humble monk had had far greater impact on the Aleut people and their culture. The Aleuts have been overwhelmingly Russian Orthodox for two centuries—an important chapter in their story.

There were never more than 800 ethnic Russians at any one time in all of Alaska. Thus, the future of this Russian colony depended on the training of Alaskans, whom the Russians called "the Americans," to assume responsibility for development of the region.

Bilingual and Christian, Aleuts sent their children to church-operated schools, so that in two generations they were producing their own college educated leadership. The first Aleut priest, Father Yakov (Jacob) Netsvetov, finished seminary in Irkutsk and returned to Alaska with his Russian wife in 1828. He spent 20 years at Atka, running the bilingual school and visiting his scattered flock along the length of the Chain and as far as the Kurile Islands, just north of Japan. After a series of personal calamities, including a house fire that destroyed his residence, and the death of his wife and the nephew they were raising as their own son, he requested retirement. Instead he was transferred to the Yukon Delta, where he learned Yup'ik and began the first bilingual school at Ikogmiut in 1844. He had to devise an orthography for this language and began translation work, some of which was eventually published fifty years later and then widely used among Orthodox Christian Yup'iks for another hundred years.

Ivan Pan'kov, an Unangan leader from Akun Island, served as translator, mentor and advisor to Father Ioan Veniaminov, the founder of the first Unangan school, who arrived in Alaska in 1823. Together they developed the Aleut alphabet, translated the Gospel according to Matthew, a catechism, and a booklet of Bible stories into Unangan.

Another "American," Ivan Kruikov, we know about from a brief note by Veniaminov who wrote of Kruikov's extraordinary artistic ability. Veniaminov observed that Kruikov only needed to look at a person for a moment, and could then withdraw to another room and return a few minutes later with a perfectly adequate portrait. Experts believe Kruikov was responsible for creating the first Aleut icons at Unalaska and that a collection of his unsigned works remains there.

The Lukin Family also gained prominence in early Russian Alaska. Simeon, the father, was rescued from Sitka and brought to Kodiak after the Tlingit destroyed that outpost in 1802, then raised under Baranov's guidance and sent to help Ivan Kolmakov operate the trading post on the middle Kuskokwim. When Kolmakov died, Simeon assumed responsibility for the trading post himself, marrying a Yup'ik and, after her death, wedding an Athabascan women. His sons, Ivan and Constantine, were raised at the outpost, where they became thoroughly familiar with the country, the Native people and their languages. The brothers eventually were appointed to assist Father Jacob Netsvetov at Ikogmiut, where they lived for nearly 20 years.

Constantine was a proficient hunter and the mission relied heavily on his talents. During one particularly severe winter, Father Jacob wrote in his pastoral journal that their food supply was nearly exhausted and that he was dispatching Constantine to find food. There were few supplies in the entire village, in fact, and many Yup'ik households were facing starvation as well. Each day Father Netsvetov noted with increasing alarm the anxiety that was gripping the town.

At the end of each year, when the annual supply and mail ship arrived, each priest would copy and seal his daily journal and send it to the bishop in Sitka, over a thousand miles away. At this particular time, a new bishop, Bishop Peter, had just arrived from St. Petersburg, a city-educated and aristocratic man who had not yet ventured into the Alaskan wilderness. Reading Netsvetov's journal, Bishop Peter began writing his own comments and reactions, like an English teacher grading a student's paper. When he came to the section in which Ikogmuit's situation was becoming increasingly desperate, he wrote on the edge of the page "Oh my God!" As the food supply dwindled, the bishop expressed his own concern, adding, "Lord have mercy!" At the end of the page, Netsvetov wrote "Thanks be to God, Constantine returned today with three caribou. We will have sufficient food until the fish return." To this, Bishop Peter questioned, "Meat during Lent?"

This is perhaps the earliest recorded evidence of a newly arrived urban Alaskan administrator oblivious to the unique circumstances faced by rural Alaskans.

Ivan Lukin probably resembled his Athabascan mother, for when the Colonial government wanted someone to investigate the British presence at Fort Yukon, they sent him up river to explore. Dressed in Indian clothes he impersonated a local fur trapper and visited the Hudson Bay post, counted the number of Englishmen in residence, got back into his canoe, paddled back downstream, and wrote a full report, in Russian, to headquarters in Sitka. This first Aleut spy was never detected. Time and again it was the ability of the Aleuts to move freely in two worlds, their familiarity with two or more languages and cultures, that made them indispensable to the Russian-American Company.

Archimandritov Ilarion, from the Alaska Peninsula, attended grade school at Unalaska and was one of the first Alaska Natives to attend the Russian Naval Academy at Kronstadt, on the Baltic Sea. Graduating with expertise in navigation and cartography, he sailed Russian American Company ships across the North Pacific and Bering Seas for several decades of the mid-1800s. After a tragic mishap that sank one of his ships, the company administration assigned him a new task, mapping the coastline of Kodiak and Cook Inlet. Archimandritov's charts were published in the Trebenkov atlas, the first to offer the world a detailed report on Alaska's geography, one of the last places on earth to be charted — and by an Aleut!

Alexander Kashevarov also attended the Kronstadt Naval Academy and sailed several times around the world on supply vessels, bringing mail, food, and European trade items to Alaska, via London, Rio de Janeiro, Tierra del Fuego, Santiago, San Francisco and Sitka. Before the construction of the Panama Canal, this was a long and dangerous voyage. Kashevarov is credited with discovering and mapping some of the Marianas Islands in the mid-nineteenth century, and for delivering emergency supplies to Ayan, on the Siberian coast, where he was for a brief time also Governor.

With Nikolai Chernov, Kashevarov took two company ships to the Point Hope area in northwest Alaska, where they got into kayaks and paddled along the coast. Mapping it as they went, they eventually reached a spot forty miles east of Barrow, where the Inuit forced the intruders to turn back.

As Major General, Alexander Kashevarov retired to St. Petersburg, where he submitted reports critical of the Russian America Company's rule of his homeland, and offered further encouragement to the Tsarist government for its transfer to American rule. The Kashevarov family also produced at least six Orthodox priests who served with distinction across the entire Alaskan diocese during the next several decades.

OPEN TO THE NEW

For over two and a half centuries the Aleutian and Kodiak regions have been swept by the winds of cultural change. The era when frontiersmen from Siberia married, traded with, and fought the indigenous peoples in Southwestern Alaska was followed by nearly 30 years of oppression and exploitation under the dictatorial rule of the Russian fur trading monopoly's manager, Alexander Baranov. Then came a profound cultural shift under the guidance of Father Ioan (St. Innocent) Veniaminov, Ivan Pan'kov, and Father (now also saint) Jacob Netsvetov, during which literate Aleuts were prepared for leadership roles throughout Alaska. Natives like Father Jacob were trained not only as clergy but as accountants, carpenters, ship builders, navigators, school teachers, paramedics, cartographers, musicians, artists and storekeepers.

After the Russian transfer of sovereignty to the United States in 1867, and continuing through the internments of World War II, this unique multi-racial, multi-lingual society was deliberately suppressed for another hundred years. But the People have endured.

The Aleut are characterized by an openness to the new and the technologically advanced. I often tell my students that the key to the Aleut "game of life" is addition. The Unangan and Sugpiaq, as well as some Yup'ik people, intermarried with Siberians, many of whom were themselves Native people, learned each others' languages, went to bilingual schools to add literacy in both languages to their résumés, and graduated with vocational and professional skills that enabled them to make positive contributions to their society while retaining the essentials of their ancient heritage. They combined the best of both worlds, eating seal stew at supper and finishing the meal with tea from a samovar. They moved freely between cultures outside their own, embracing the idea that more is better.

While the traditional hierarchic patriarchy of ancient times survived into the middle of the twentieth century, the great disruption created by the sudden forced evacuation of the Unangan people during the Second World War virtually eliminated the last vestiges of the ancient leadership patterns. The Alutiiq and Unangan languages survived into the 1950s, and in some communities even into the 1970s, but few young people speak either language today, despite over a century and a half of literacy in both Native languages.

Now, pride in the ancient culture is resurgent. A revival of song and dance as well as language has begun throughout the Aleutian and Kodiak Archipelagos. Summer culture camps there perpetuate traditional skills and practices that link the People to their ancient homeland, to their ancestors, and to each other.

Fortunately, literate Aleuts wrote and even published their own stories and translations four generations ago. "The Mink Boy" included here, was recorded at Karluk around 1905. Although Veniaminov collected only three old stories and five old songs at Unalaska in the 1820s, complaining at that early time that so much had already been forgotten, Jochelson uncovered dozens more myths and legends in the region nearly a hundred years later.

Like the Mink Boy, the Aleut people used the tools available to them and adapted to their circumstances. Instead of falling into the tragic dilemma of being forced to choose between one or the other, an "either/or" that has no healthy solution, the Aleut people responded "both/and." This strength allowed them not only to survive, but eventually to regain control of their lives and to influence in positive ways the cultures of other Native Alaskans. Aleuts mapped the coastlines, introduced schooling to Yup'iks and ran most of the businesses in Sitka. They served as sea captains, bringing trade goods and supplies to the trading company's outposts, vaccinated villagers against smallpox, translated books, built churches and opened schools. And when rule of Alaska passed from Russia to the United States, they provided political leadership, standing up courageously and demanding equality and justice for themselves and all Alaska Natives.

The Aleut Story is a saga of adaptation: eagerly accepting, adding on to what they had already known and resisting pressure to subtract—to abandon—what they had already embraced. The Cultural Story of the Aleuts has many chapters, many layers. These pages are a very short introduction into the rich and fascinating heritage of a remarkable, resilient People—always "good at addition, but not subtraction." Such is their genius.

Driving at Dutch Harbor. *Photo by Bill Hess*

THE MINK BOY: AN ALUTIIQ STORY

(Based on a story recorded by Frank Golder on Kodiak Island, ca. 1900)

A grandmother and her grandson lived alone along a rocky beach overlooking the ocean. The grandmother was getting older and weaker and could no longer conduct all the hunting and gathering necessary to feed the two of them. The grandson, on the other hand, was growing stronger, becoming capable of doing some of the work. Grandmother prepared everything he would need – his harpoon, his spears, his bow and arrows, his poisoned darts – and then told him one morning: "It is time for you to begin hunting for us. Your kayak is ready. Your weapons are ready. You are ready. But you must be careful not to enter certain dangerous places. Do not climb that mountain there, in the distance. Do not even touch it. Stay away from that mountain!"

The boy indicated his agreement by raising his eyebrows.

"And another thing," grandmother added. "Do not enter that forest. Stay away from that forest. Never go into it."

The boy nodded his assent.

"And finally," the grandmother ordered, "do not venture into that bay. Whatever you do, do not paddle into that bay. Stay out of that bay at all costs!"

And the lad agreed not to enter the bay either.

As he was about to leave, the grandmother stopped him, called him back, and handed him an old, dried piece of leather. The boy looked at the shriveled up skin and asked what it was.

"It's an old mink skin!" she informed him. "An old mink skin!"

"Well, what is it used for? Why are you giving it to me?" the boy asked.

"Just in case," Grandmother replied.

"In case of what?"

"In case you get yourself into any kind of trouble. In case you have any emergencies, you can use it."

"How will this help in an emergency?" the confused boy wondered.

"Well, if you find yourself in any kind of difficulty," grandmother continued, "you must chew on this skin, soften it, stretch it and pull it over your head."

"Okay." And the boy stuffed the old mink skin into his parka and paddled off. He went straight to the mountain he was forbidden to touch or climb. He beached his kayak and began the ascent. Half way up the slope, the earth quaked, and with a loud rumbling crash, a landslide buried him alive.

The boy frantically tried to extricate himself from the mud and stones that covered him. Exhausted and fearing he was about to die, he suddenly remembered the old mink skin. He pulled it out of his parka and began chewing on it, stretching it. When at last he pulled it over his head, he was instantly transformed into a mink. In mink form he was able to burrow his way out to the surface.

Happy to be saved from this catastrophe, he removed the skin, became a boy again and resumed his adventures, going straight to the forest he was not supposed to enter. Before long, he was attacked by a bear. The bear chased him through the forest and when he was about to be caught and certainly eaten alive, he remembered the mink skin once more, chewed on it, stretched it, pulled it over his head and became, in an instant, a tiny mink. The bear was perplexed, not realizing that the boy had not vanished but had merely changed his shape. In the form of a mink, the boy silently disappeared into the brush, hurried to the beach, removed the skin, returned to the shape of a boy once more, and quickly paddled away—in the direction of the forbidden bay.

Here a family of bowhead whales were feeding and playing and it occurred to the boy that if he could harvest one he would not have to hunt again for a very long time. One whale would feed him and *his grandmother for many months. But there were monsters in this bay as well. One spotted the boy, chasing him onto the beach where he hid in a cave all night long, hungry, tired and very wet.*

In the morning, he took the poisoned darts that his grandmother had provided him and returned to the water in the form of a mink. He carefully inserted the darts in the hide of the sleeping monster as he lay near the beach, and successfully killed the one who had tried to eat him. Not having any more darts for his whale hunt, he decided to return home, happy to have survived the three ordeals, though without any food for his grandmother.

As he turned his kayak homeward, he came to a huge lake, teeming with happy, plump, contented mink. He pulled out the mink skin and chewed on it. Stretching it and pulling it over his head, he changed himself into a mink one more time. And he is there to this day.

NOTES

The story, of a type similar to many cultures, begins with an elder and a youth in isolation. No background information is provided to explain how they were left alone, far from any community. The elder is experienced and wise and offers sensible advice to the boy. The boy, being a human teenager, is respectful enough not to argue with the elder, but has plans of his own. Kids, as modern advertisers have discovered, don't hear "don't." Put up a sign that reads "Don't do drugs," and you have just brought to everyone's attention the very behavior you are trying to discourage. "Don't Smoke" says "Smoke!" "Don't Drink" says "Drink!" So the boy being told "Don't go up that mountain," or "Don't enter that bay" is really being tempted to do what he has just been told not to. And the wise grandmother knows this too. That is why she foresees the need to provide the boy with the magical mink skin.

The grandmother's admonition also reflects a motif found in stories from cultures all over the world, that of the "one forbidden thing" — a taboo established in the beginning of a story so that it may be broken, bringing the story's lesson to light. The sea lions' instruction to Naatsilanei not to think of the past on his journey home, or God's order to Eve not to eat from a certain tree, are other examples of stories that employ this device.

Being transformed, or "shapeshifting" into an animal, is a curse found often in European folklore. Beauty and the Beast, the Frog Prince and other such stories describe how a wicked witch or cruel sorcerer has changed a human being into an animal. In the Frog Prince, only the first kiss of true love can change the Prince back into a man, so he can marry the Princess and live "happily ever after."

But in Native American stories, being turned into an animal is rarely all bad news. Except for their outward appearance, animals in these stories tend to be much like humans, albeit usually wiser. They see things humans cannot see, hear what humans cannot hear, smell what humans cannot smell. They know things humans do not know and can do things humans cannot do. Besides this, they share information. They cooperate across the boundaries of their species. In many ways, animals are superior, not inferior, to humans. All of this is understood in traditional cultures.

The boy is saved repeatedly by his ability to change himself into a mink, and in the end decides to remain as a mink, and live "happily ever after."

THE ORIGIN OF SEA OTTERS

AN UNANGAN STORY

There was once a leading and highly respected Unangan man who had a wife, a proficient and courageous son, and a teenage daughter. His children were his pride and joy. Everyone knew how much he delighted and rejoiced in his son and his daughter.

Now the daughter's time for seclusion arrived and her father built her a small house, where she stayed alone, as is the custom of the Human Beings when a girl transforms from a child into a woman. No one but a serving maid entered this house during her initiation. The maid brought food several times a day.

During their seclusion, such girls are very powerful. They must be careful about what they say and what they look at, for their words and their gaze carry great consequences. If they say the wrong thing or even look at what is forbidden, the whole world will change, the balance of nature will be upset, catastrophe may follow not only for her, but for her family and community.

While the girl was away, her brother began to hunt sea birds, and he often did so at night. No one thought this strange, because some animals must be hunted after dark, and this young man was always successful. The animals favored him and gave themselves to him.

In the dark of night, the daughter began to receive a visitor who pleaded with her, begged her to love him and to allow him to love her. This was absolutely forbidden and the girl considered

shamed, the brother does not seek treatment immediately, but crawls around in the dark and suffers so much loss of blood that he dies.

The sister summons all her powers to revive her brother and expose his crime to the family and community. She manages to bring him back to life, but he has not learned his lesson. She is forced to flee from him and they both perish, each in their own best parkas. He does not gain his desire, for she plunges to her death rather than allow him to touch her again. As sea otters, they migrate in opposite directions, for even sea mammals do not mate with their own family members. Because they both dove in wearing their most beautiful regalia — hers designed to celebrate her life-giving powers, and his to be worn at death — the sea otters sport the finest coats of all the animals who swim in the sea.

Top: Aleut girls dancing.

Left: Aleut children.

Photos by Bill Hess

Preceding page: Inupiat drummer.

Top: Watching for whales at a hunter blind.

Bottom: Inupiat dancer.

Photos by Bill Hess

CYCLES OF LIFE, OF LIGHT AND DARKNESS

It is generally thought that Canada's Inuit culture originated in Alaska, spreading across the Arctic during the last five millennia, migrating as far east as Greenland. The Inupiat, often collectively called "Eskimo," are the people most Americans conjure up when they think of Alaska.

The Inupiat live with months of perpetual night and months of perpetual daylight in the northernmost and coldest environment on the continent. In Labrador and Greenland the Inuit invented the igloo as a temporary shelter—their way of pitching a tent for the night.

It is believed that the Inupiat gave life to many of the languages spoken to the south and east. The variety of Eskimo languages and cultures in Alaska provides supporting evidence for the theory that Alaska was the original home of many northern indigenous nations, for when it comes to the origin of language, variety points to the source. For example, if a linguist who knew nothing about the history of the United States visited both the Atlantic and Pacific coasts, he or she could quickly determine that English speakers first settled along the Atlantic seaboard, and later migrated westward. The greatest variety of accents and dialects occurs from Maine to Florida, while there is hardly a distinctive local speech pattern between Seattle and San Diego. As the settlers moved west, English mixed and "homogenized" so that today far less variety can be found along the West Coast. In the same way, the many distinct Eskimo languages that originated in Alaska became more blended during the eastward migrations.

All traditional cultures have to be adaptive and creative, exploiting the resources of their ecosystem in order to survive. From a European perspective, the Inupiat had the least resources and the smallest chance of success. Since their natural environment is generally treeless, they had no locally grown wood for construction of homes or for heat. No totem poles stand here. The North Slope of Alaska is an Arctic desert with very little annual precipitation. Vegetation grows close to the ground. The radical change of seasons forces many summer visitors to the high Arctic to migrate southward or to sleep through a winter night that in the farthest north begins in November and lasts until February. In the age before Edison, how do you work, play, eat, survive in three months of darkness? Why didn't they move south?

Like traditional cultures elsewhere, the Inupiat believe they are meant to live where they are, and that they have been provided all they need to occupy the vast stretch of homeland given to them by Raven when the world was new. Subsistence hunting and gathering depends heavily on sea mammals, especially whales, who provide entire communities with meat and oil, food and heat during the three moons of winter. A good whaling season means sufficient food for the winter and demands that the Real People offer ceremonial thanks to the "Inua" of the animals, permitting the spirits of those who have offered themselves to the Human Beings to be reborn.

Like their Yup'it cousins, the Inupiat see themselves as the guardians of their world, receiving the animals as food and clothing and conducting the appropriate rites to assure the harmonious ecological balance of the cosmos.

The Inupiat at Point Hope, on the Bering Sea, tell a story of the origins of their land. When the world was young, the peninsula on which their community stands was not there. But a great hunter, a mythic hero they call Raven Man, harpooned a whale, perhaps the first whale, and brought it to the surface as he sang to it, coaxing it with his floats, to rise. The land on which the village stands is the body of that ancient bowhead. The whale sustains and nourishes, whether it offers itself on the sea, or in the resources hunted and gathered on the shore. It is all whale. Everything is whale. Life is whale. Birds, geese, ducks, squirrels, seals, walrus, caribou—all these serve to tide the community over until the whales come.

Like the Yup'ik, the Inupiaq home is built in the shape of the Eskimo Universe, and the stories indicate passages from a normal to a supernatural plane, the principal characters leaving or returning through the usual door or smoke hole, the passage to another dimension. This cosmic structure of the building sets the stage for the ceremonial life of the People—for the spirits of the animals, their Inua, must be treated respectfully, thanked with humility, and returned to their proper home for a period of gestation, in order to be reborn.

In this cycle, the role of the women, who remain in their dwellings while the men are hunting, is considered essential to the hunt. By performing the appropriate rituals of respect, the women invite and lure the whales to return, to offer themselves to the Human Beings, and then pass onward into the realm of the spirits, in order to be incarnated once more. If the rituals are not followed, if the rites of respect and gratitude are not performed, the very survival of the People is endangered, for everything depends on the Sacred Gift of Whale.

A whaling crew on the Bering Sea traditionally was composed of eight hunters—a leader and his seven crew members. The leader provides food to his men, who camp on the ice awaiting the first sign of the whales, as soon as the winter ice begins to open. Traditionally, umiaks, large open boats made of sea mammal skins stretched over a delicate wooden frame, had to be dragged carefully out to the leads (breaks in the ice) and launched as soon as there was sufficient water to float them. Then the long watch would begin. The crew had to be careful about how they talked, what they ate and where they put their garbage, for the whales could be offended by human misconduct and would avoid disrespectful men.

The women back in the village had to observe certain rites of respect as well, and their behavior traditionally determined the success of the hunt even more than how their husbands conducted themselves. For this reason, a whale was referred to as being the whale of the captain's wife, rather than of the captain. As in most traditional societies, the spiritual power resided within the ladies. According to the Inupiat, it was an old woman, the first human, who created the Raven Man, a remarkable character who plays the role of Raven in many similar Tlingit stories. It is the Raven Man, for example, who steals the daylight, which a powerful, perhaps "rich" man, had carefully concealed in his home. The world, at the beginning, was dark and Raven Man had to steal the Light, release it into the world, and produce the first dawn. He uses deception and strength in every version of this story to enlighten the world. In the Tlingit version, Raven himself becomes human, entering the body of the Rich Man's daughter by stowing away as a spruce needle that she unknowingly drinks, in order to be born as a child, the Rich Man's grandson. The Rich Man spoils his grandson, giving him everything he demands, until the boy insists on playing with the containers that hold the stars, the moon, and finally the sun.

In the Inupiaq legend, as it is told in Northwest Alaska, the Raven Man entices the daughter of the owner to do the same, then, snatching the prize from her, flees from the house with the owner in chase. When Raven Man releases daylight into the world, the Rich Man releases darkness, so that one would counteract the other forever. This is the Inupiaq universe.

Understandably, a people living in a world that is dark and cold for months, then filled with light and life for an equally long time, perceive a universe composed of opposite and even antagonistic forces. There are spirits, ghosts, monsters, mythical and natural creatures whose unexpected interventions can upset and even end our lives. Life is precarious, filled with danger, suffering, loss, pain, and at any moment, death. Expect the unexpected seems to be a cardinal feature of the Inupiaq way of seeing reality. The unpredictable character of the world seems to dominate the stories of the Inupiat more than any other culture in Alaska. Here the stories are filled with transformations, of people, animals and weird creatures changing shape, revealing a new and unexpected side, becoming something new. Nothing is what it seems. Everything and everyone possess multiple levels of awareness, and contain unexplored depths of meaning, of reality. It is a fantastic world.

From the basic forms in the traditional stories children learn about what to expect and how to cope with the realities of life. The great cycles of life, of light and darkness, the long Arctic night giving way to a long Arctic day, decay and death followed by renewal and rebirth, constitute the themes of Inupiaq ceremonial life. At the winter solstice, the People invoke the Dawn and the re-creation of the world in public rituals, singing and feasting, commemorating

Nalukataq, the Inupiat blanket toss. *Photo by Bill Hess*

and participating in the sacred time of those First Days. Each year restarts the cycle of rebirth; this new beginning is possible in part because the Humans are performing their rituals and invoking renewal—of the cosmos, of the animals, and of themselves.

Bering Sea Eskimo culture, which centers on the reverence, gratitude and respect the People must render the spirits of the animals, has produced remarkable art depicting these Inua, not only on ceremonial regalia, masks, rattles and drums, but on everyday hunting and cooking implements. The Smithsonian Institute in Washington D.C. houses a remarkable collection gathered by ethnologist Edward Nelson over a century ago. Named the "Man who buys good-for-nothing things" by the locals, he collected thousands of artifacts that now constitute the core of the national museum's Eskimo treasures.

Bucket handles, knives, harpoons, bowls and ladles are all adorned with images of the whale. Where driftwood was difficult or impossible to obtain, the frames of their very homes, their miniature worlds, were constructed of whale ribs. The Real People not only depend on whales for food and fuel, but live on a land that was itself a whale, and live inside a whale all their lives. The World is a Whale!

There are two extraordinary films produced several decades ago by the Alaska Native Film Project, headed by Leonard Kamerling, based at the University of Alaska Fairbanks, focusing on Bering Sea whaling culture on St. Lawrence Island. "On Spring Ice" and "At the Time of Whaling" include elders speaking to teens and children about their whaling traditions, telling stories in their ancestral language with English subtitles. The most amazing scene I recall shows a whaling crew, with a small outboard motor attached to the stern of their umiak, approaching a whale. The bowhead is huge, dwarfing the little skin boat by ten times its length. But Whale waits. It could dive. It could swim away faster than the hunters could possibly paddle. It could attack. But it only waits, quietly and patiently for the harpoons to fly. The whale, as the traditional peoples of Alaska will always affirm, gives itself to the People. The documentary videos provide evidence that this appears to be so.

In traditional times, the long dark months were the season for story telling, singing and ceremonial gatherings. The Real People must return certain parts of the sea mammals through the ice to reassure the Inua of their respect and gratitude and prompt the animals to return and offer themselves again. As with Alaska's other indigenous groups, the "curriculum" of the traditional educational system in Inupiaq culture is rooted in sacred stories that reveal the permanent structures and the appropriate paradigms, the patterns, for human behavior. The stories are filled with characters who either lived and survived by observing the proper rites and gestures, or suffered and perished because they failed to conform to these eternal structures and norms. Art and song reinforce the same patterns. Ceremony animates the old stories making them come "alive," drawing the community into them. The shaman, who, it was universally believed, had recaptured some of the lost abilities of the First People, could ascend into the spirit world above this one, or descend into the spirit world beneath it, and return possessing a personal familiarity with the Realities about which the old stories speak. Shamans were thereby able to deal with the spirits, the Inua, communicating if not with all of them, at least with some. This ability to connect with these powers endowed shamans with healing as well as prophetic abilities.

Certainly there were some shamans who were quacks, imposters, fakes, but there are also many credible accounts of shamans who could heal the sick, who accurately prescribed how to find food, find lost objects or people, and who were skilled at bringing relationships back into balance. You can fool some of the people some of the time, but you can't fool all of the people all of the time. By successfully dealing with what traditional Inupiat believed to be spiritual imbalances and crises, the shamans provided an essential mediatory service to their communities. Their prophetic and healing abilities validated the traditional world view. Many Inuit stories relate the magical and fantastic abilities of shamans who had regained some of the lost talents and abilities of the First People, and who understood what the animals were saying, thus enjoying free access to other levels of Reality.

Many Inupiaq stories are tragic and violent; others are filled with the mysterious, the illogical, the totally unexpected, reflecting their Arctic Reality, looking along their unique beam of bright, intense, but limited sunlight.

HOW PEOPLE GOT FIRE

A LEGEND FROM THE NORTH SLOPE

*O*n *a river lived a man, his wife and their only son. When he was a very young child his mother made him two little dolls, a man and a woman, and these were his only toys. He would often pretend that they were alive, and together they held ceremonies and dances, as the boy used his imagination to entertain himself in their house, far from other people and other playmates.*

Further upstream there was a village the son visited to listen to stories. There he learned of the man who owned fire. The world was still a warm place, but it was getting colder every year. People, mostly hunters, went further and further up the river to find the man with fire, but they never returned. The boy wondered where they went, what happened to them, and why they never came back.

The boy had an uncle in this village, and many cousins. Maybe it was this uncle who gave the boy a magic charm he always wore around his neck. The boy visited his uncle's house for weeks at a time, always asking about the Man who has Fire, but no one had any further information. They explained that since no one had ever come back from there, they knew nothing about the man, where exactly he lived or how he kept the fire. The boy began asking elders in the village what they knew about the Man with Fire, but they all answered the same way, pleading ignorance. Finally the son went to visit the oldest man in the village. This ancient man told him that the Man with Fire lived an incredibly long distance away, near a place where huge boulders formed a chain across the river. The wise elder expressed his opinion that those who left to find the Man with Fire never got to his house because it was such a long and difficult journey. But the old man also knew where the trail to this place began and showed it to the boy.

That autumn, the son decided he would depart his home and begin the long trek to the Man with Fire's house. He was prepared to spend years, if necessary, to find this place and bring fire back to the People. He took with him his dolls, and the magical charm, the amulet he wore around his neck that would permit him to change his shape if he needed to.

He walked all fall and all winter, stopping only when he had to find food, or when he needed to rest, but never for very long. He walked all spring and all summer and into the next autumn. By the end of the second year he knew he was getting close to the place the old man had described, but it was still beyond the horizon. At the end of the third year, he arrived at the river and walked down to the beach.

According to the way the old man had described the place, the house in which the Man with Fire lived should be on the other side. Leaping from one huge rock to the other with great effort he managed to cross the river. The hill leading up from the riverbank was covered with old and broken weapons – evidence that many others had arrived at this shore and had been defeated or killed here by the Man with Fire. As he reached the top of the first hill, he saw how the land fell downward, then rose again. On the second hill stood the house of the Man with Fire.

Just then the Man with Fire came out of his house and looked directly toward the son. The boy dropped to the ground and hid behind a large bump of tundra. The terrain was covered with little pillows of earth, soft and pliable, blanketed in moss, grass and berries. The boy reasoned, "I'll be too easily spotted if I remain in the form of a boy," so he used the amulet around his neck to turn himself into a ground squirrel.

In the shape of a squirrel, the boy approached the house carefully, quietly, stealthily. But progress was slow. He raised his head above the tundra to investigate and immediately the Man with Fire came out and looked around again. Seeing nothing, he went back in, while the Squirrel Boy continued his slow advance. Again and again overwhelmed by suspicion, the man would suddenly rush out of house to take a look, but again and again saw nothing.

The Squirrel Boy realized that even as a small animal, he could be easily spotted and killed, so he decided to change his form again. Using his amulet, he changed himself into a feather, a tiny piece of duck down. Now, however, he was at the mercy of the wind, and the breeze was not blowing constantly or very strongly at this time. At last, the wind lifted him into the air, but he floated high above the river, the tundra and the house, his destination. The wind blew him in every direction. Finally, after some time, he landed directly in front of the house.

The Man with Fire never heard him arrive and did not come out to investigate because the boy as a feather was so light and so small. Using his magic once more, the boy returned to human form, but still the Man with Fire did not come out.

Great!, thought the boy. He sneaked up to the window and even dared to open it. Still the Man with Fire did not hear him and did not react. The boy saw the Man sitting in the house, facing the entrance, with a lamp filled with fire on his lap.

"Now I need to distract him," thought the boy. "I will remain very quiet, but I will use those two old dolls my mother gave me as decoys." The boy put the dolls on the windowsill and they began dancing, but without any need for the boy to hold them. They danced by themselves, like puppets without strings. Surprised, the Man with Fire looked up, and laughed. "Go ahead and dance! Dance all you want! Leap and dance and have a great time!"

Knowing that the Man with Fire was enjoying the dancing dolls, the boy went right into the house. He grabbed the lamp from the man's lap and ran out the door before the Man with Fire had a chance to realize what had happened. The boy raced down the first *hill and up the second, with the Man chasing him and yelling, "If I catch you, I'll kill you! I'll kill you like I killed all those others!"*

The boy got to the rocks and began leaping from one to the other, crossing the river as fast as he could, still carrying the lamp and balancing it carefully. At the shore, the Man stopped and called to him, "All right! I can't jump over these rocks. You can keep the fire. But you cannot keep it for yourself. You must share it with all the People!"

The son began his journey homeward and, after three more years, arrived safely. It was autumn and the People needed fire now more than ever. Each year the weather had been getting colder and they could not have lived many more years without the light and heat that the fire brought into their lives.

The boy was not a boy any more, but a young man. He had been gone for six years. He entered the village and gave fire to his uncle. Then he went home, brought fire to his parents, and lived there the rest of his days. That is how Human Beings got fire.

NOTES

Fire theft is a universal theme in traditional mythology. Nearly every culture has a story about how fire was brought to the world. The Tlingit story describes how Raven did it. This story, reportedly told at Barrow and shared among the people in Point Hope and Kotzebue, seems to have circulated widely among the Inupiaq.

The boy was accustomed to being alone, playing alone, and received necessary basic instruction and power from his parents. He received additional instruction and power from his uncle. And he got a lot of advice and guidance from an elder. This is the traditional educational pattern. But he has to apply these lessons to the challenges of his own life and take responsibility for the direction he takes.

Being able to change into an animal and even an inanimate object worked to the boy's advantage. The notion here is that even feathers can have a kind of consciousness, that the whole of nature is aware and sensitive, and that humans must interact with their world with care, sensitivity and humility.

There is something like a "Jack in the Beanstalk" flavor to the ending of this tale, with the Man chasing the boy who has stolen his treasure. But the final command of the Man that the boy must share what he has discovered is typically Inupiaq. It is the quiet boy who listened to what his parents, uncle and elders taught who succeeded where many stronger and overconfident warriors had failed.

BROTHERS IN THE STORM

A LEGEND FROM ST. LAWRENCE ISLAND

There once were five brothers who spent their days tending a reindeer herd that had belonged to their father. They were far from the village when a sudden winter storm burst upon them. In a few moments they found themselves completely enshrouded in thick blowing snow, the flakes so large and coming so fast that they could not see their own feet. As the wind howled and the snow deepened, they began to panic. Suddenly, the oldest brother began singing. His lyrics meant, "It is against the deer and against those of us who are walking." As he continued to sing, the wind calmed, the clouds parted and they found themselves near a dwelling.

It was a very large house, a traditional semi-subterranean sod house, and as the snow subsided they began crawling, groping around it to find the entrance. Once they found the door, they crawled through the passage and entered the main room of the house. The interior was warm and dry and they were grateful to have stumbled in from the blizzard outside.

Silently sitting in the far corner of this room was a little old lady who shouted "Who is there?" Her surprise was genuine, since this house was far from any other habitation and she had never before received guests. "If not even birds come to this house, who can be here?" she demanded.

The oldest brother answered, "We are your nephews. Our father always told us about you and now we have come to visit. Our father, your brother, assured us that you were kind and hospitable. He told us you would offer us protection if we ever needed it!"

The old lady replied, "Well, if my brother said those nice things about me, please, come in!"

Her guests were covered with ice and snow and exhausted from being out in the storm. They were delighted to be invited into the house but their parkas were soon dripping as the snow and ice melted in the warm interior.

"Take off your wet clothing," their hostess ordered, "and I'll take care of it."

They were glad to get out of their soggy boots and parkas and quickly piled them up on the floor in the main room, just inside the entrance to the house.

The little old lady prepared supper for them and they all ate their fill. Then she told them to go to bed.

"All of you go to sleep now, and don't get up until morning. If you wake up before I tell you, stay in bed. Do not get out of bed until I tell you it is time."

So all the brothers went to bed and tried to go straight to sleep. The older four managed to fall asleep right away, but the youngest was curious and could not sleep. He listened to the weather. The wind was quieting down. As the hours passed, he eventually could not hear any wind blowing at all. As dawn approached, he got more and more curious about what was happening outside. So he sneaked out of bed and peeked out the door. Everything was warm and sunny that morning. The sky was nearly cloudless, the wind completely calm. And up in the sky was the little old lady, clearing the heavens with her skin scraper. There was only one tiny cloud left and she was about to eliminate it. The boy watched in amazement as the old lady began struggling with this last cloud. No matter how hard she scraped, she could not remove it. It was as if the cloud had become like a rock, hard and impossible to break apart.

The old lady became a bit frustrated and eventually exhausted trying to eliminate this final cloud. In her weariness, she glanced down to the house and, spotting the boy peeking out the door, descended immediately to the entrance. Furious, she charged *angrily into the house. "I told you to stay in bed! I told you not to get up! You should not have come to spy on me! Now that final cloud will always be there. I had intended to get rid of all the clouds so that you would have a nice, sunny world, but now there will always be storms."*

The other brothers awoke and quickly put on their already dried boots and coats. They hurried home and arrived safely. But they never found that old lady or her house ever again.

NOTES

Stories about many brothers, the oldest as wiser and the leader of the others, and the youngest as disobedient and foolish, can be found in many cultures. Sometimes the youngest emerges as the wisest as he undergoes several initiatory experiences, sometimes he becomes the image of foolishness.

The sudden ferocious storm warns that such weather can change and envelop hunters at almost any time. It is an unpredictable and dangerous world. The "little old lady" may be the first Human, since in Arctic Eskimo cultures, a woman served as the original Human Being.

First People always have powers that far surpass modern humans. Her house may be the original universe, warm and dry, a sort of Paradise that pre-existed the world as we experience it now, filled with cold, darkness and violence.

It is traditionally appropriate to address older women as "aunts" or "grandmothers," and older men as "uncles" or "grandfathers" as titles of respect, identifying them as more experienced, wiser and of superior rank. Men of the same older generation introduce their friends to their own children as "your uncle" or "your grandfather" and women refer to their peers as "your aunts" or "your grandmothers" when speaking to their children. The village is a huge extended family in which everyone is related.

In the story, the older brothers obey the elder's instructions, but the youngest boy allows his curiosity to tempt him into disregarding her explicit warnings. Because he did not obey, the world will always be stormy. Refusal to conform, to submit to the wise injunctions of elders, can bring negative personal, or even collective, consequences.

Preceding page: Athabascans elders. *Photo by Bill Hess*

Top: Yup'ik dancers of Scammon Bay. *Photo by James Barker*

Bottom: Athabascan square dancers. *Photo by Bill Hess*

HOLDING ON TO ALL THAT IS GOOD

In the history of intercultural and interracial relationships in North America, the Inupiaq appear in one of the most recent chapters. The first act in our national story, beginning at about 1500 and continuing for three hundred years, was characterized by violence. Historically, this is the way tribal peoples everywhere have been treated by intruders: the safest and most permanent way to resolve conflicts with anyone racially or culturally different is to kill them. "The only good Indian is a..." Even third grade students in Alaskan schools can complete the saying accurately: "...dead Indian." There is a 300-year-long history behind that 19th Century proverb.

However, during Thomas Jefferson's administration, the government seriously reconsidered Indian policy. Having acquired the Louisiana Territories, which added thousands of square miles and hundreds of new indigenous tribes, Jefferson sought to reformulate policy toward those who were racially and culturally different from the colonists. The trans-Atlantic slave trade was abolished. No more Africans could be legally imported into the United States. Freed slaves would be shipped to West Africa, where they would found their own country, design their own flag, and write their own constitution. Liberia was born, with its capital named "Monrovia," after James Monroe, Jefferson's successor and friend.

Indian tribes were to be relocated westward. The Cherokee, in the most infamous application of the new removal policy, were relocated to Oklahoma, forced to walk the thousand-mile Trail of Tears under military escort. Over the next several decades, northern tribes were resettled in South Dakota, southern tribes in Oklahoma, for the U.S. Government considered these barren territories worthless. They promised to respect Indian use and occupancy of these areas, until, of course, gold was discovered in one and oil in the other. Removal, apartheid, segregation remain options for societies in which racial or cultural minorities compete with the majority culture.

After the Civil War, the U.S. faced a new set of problems. Hundreds of thousands of young men had died in the four-year conflict. Many more had been wounded and disabled. Insufficient manpower was available to resume the major projects that had been suspended during the war. Railroad track needed to be laid. Mines shafts needed to be drilled. Factories needed to be manned, and there were not enough White men to do the job on this side of the Atlantic. So the American people accepted the gift of the Statue of Liberty from the people of France and invited the immigration of the "tired" and "poor," the "huddled masses yearning to breath free," to the United States.

In the next half-century, nearly 18 million immigrants arrived, resulting in a new cycle of oppression. Prior to the Civil War, the descendents of the Mayflower pilgrims had held sway over national affairs. To be truly "American" and enjoy all the rights of citizenship, one needed to be Caucasian, English speaking, well trained in standards of hygiene, punctuality and social graces, and Christian in the Protestant tradition. These were the attributes of the original colonists, and those who shared their world view. They understood and played the same game of life as they had, identified with the same story, were acknowledged and accepted as full citizens in the Republic. Those who were racially different were excluded from membership in or coverage by the national covenant. America identified itself as a WASP (White, Anglo-Saxon, Protestant) and male dominated society.

The problem, for the vast majority of immigrants who arrived after 1870, was that few were WASPs. The Mediterranean folks looked a little too brown. Not many spoke English and most were Catholic. Lacking a German (Saxon) sense of time, punctuality and appropriate hygiene, the peasants from Eastern and Southern Europe were called "urban barbarians" in the Anglo press. Editors warned that unless these new savages were trained quickly to behave as civilized men, the republic would soon collapse, overwhelmed by a tide of illiteracy, poverty and alien ways that would destroy American society from within.

Inviting the workers to immigrate had seemed like a positive and creative solution to the country's labor shortage, but now that these Italians and Hungarians, Greeks and Arabs, Russians and Turks had arrived, the nation was having serious second thoughts.

The immigrants of this era were caught between two powerful historical forces: exploitative capitalism, unrestrained by a laissez faire government, and the reformist impulses of New England Protestants, who subscribed to the assimilationist theory of social organization.

On one hand, immigrant labor was cruelly exploited. Children worked in mines and factories, women in sweatshops, and men in conditions scarcely imaginable today.

On the other hand, the reformists of the day campaigned for universal education, and encouraged new laws to require all children to attend school and learn very systematically how to act and think like "real Americans." If we all did not come on the Mayflower, we should at least wish we had and act accordingly!

The assimilation of minorities into the proverbial "Melting Pot" became the new national faith, and began the second chapter in American inter-cultural relations. For the next century this approach seemed highly successful. Most Caucasian immigrants were eager to be accepted, to fit in, to have their children adopt America as their new and permanent homeland. And within a generation or two, most had successfully made the transition to citizenship and employment in American society. They could accept this new identity because that was the purpose of their coming in the first place. Their parents had decided to leave their ancestral homes and open a new chapter in the family's history. Their assimilation into American culture did not threaten the survival of their ancestral heritage, for the homeland contained millions who would preserve their language, poetry, literature, folk music and cuisine. In this sense, the immigrants were free to assimilate guiltlessly into the new culture.

For Native Americans, assimilation was a rather different experience than that of European immigrants. In the late 1800s, under the leadership of President Grant, federal Indian Policy also shifted toward assimilation and away from overt extermination and removal.

The Society of Friends ("Quakers") volunteered to participate in an experiment in Minnesota. Noting that the federal government never had sufficient funds to support schools on Indian Reservations, the Quaker missionaries proposed that they pool their resources and jointly provide schooling to the Indians, guaranteeing that the teachers would be honest and dedicated, and demanding no more funding than Congress had authorized. Strapped for funds and rocked by numerous scandals, the Grant Administration was delighted to find so easy a solution to the financial shortfall on the frontier.

The Quakers' experiment in Minnesota was soon deemed successful, and in the next several years, tribes in the "Lower 48" were divided among competing American Protestant denominations.

When Dr. Sheldon Jackson, Presbyterian minister and federal bureaucrat, was assigned the task of organizing schools in the Alaska Territory, he merely imported a philosophy and a structure that had already been developed elsewhere. He reportedly met with various American Protestant leaders and divided Alaska into religious "spheres of influence" to avoid competition and conflict between them. The Presbyterians took Southeast Alaska, and assumed responsibility for the North Slope and St. Lawrence Island as well. The Episcopalians claimed the interior, where they had already been active, having entered the upper Yukon River valley from Canada back in the Russian era. The Baptists were awarded Kodiak Island, the Methodists the Aleutians, the Lutherans and Quakers the Seward Peninsula, and the Moravian Brethren the Bristol Bay region. Each assumed responsibility for providing assimilationist educational services in their region, subsidized in part by the federal government and in part by their church's missionary society. The entire arrangement was blatantly unconstitutional, but no one challenged it for a half century.

One can only imagine how confusing and comical the construction of a school facility and the arrival of the first missionary teachers must have been in the Inupiaq region. The first curious event would have been the unexpected arrival of a ton or more of precut lumber. On the treeless coasts of the Bering Sea, driftwood was a blessing and a gift; no one had ever imagined the possibility of so much straight, clear, evenly-milled wood.

It is not hard to picture the elders gathering around the newly off-loaded lumber.

"What is this stuff?" puzzles one.

"It's wood," exclaims another, knocking his fist against it.

The wood immediately begins disappearing into the community to brace a sagging ceiling, reinforce a doorway, or to be transformed into a new harpoon.

A few weeks later, here comes the missionary construction team. Real People gather around to watch, as a new rectangular classroom building with an angular roof ascends.

"What are you building there?" they inquire.

"This is your new school," the carpenters reply.

The word "skuuluuq" enters the local vocabulary. Since, as was often the case, the new skuuluuq stands over a pre-existing well, it is assumed a "skuuluuq" is a funny-shaped wooden building meant to shelter the community's water supply. No local resident yet understands what this word "skuuluuq" means.

Then, a few weeks later, the teaching couple, almost everywhere a husband and wife recruited by the denomination to serve in the mission field, arrives. Stepping onto the beach, the man strikes the Real People as quite a remarkable sight. Sickly pale, with facial hair springing from the skin under his nose, some villagers remark on his resemblance to the walrus. Since buttons had in decades past been used as money, it is assumed this guy must be wealthy. He is covered in buttons! He has buttons on his shirt, on his vest, on his jacket and even up his sleeves. He has buttons on the spats that cover his shoes as well. The Real People wonder aloud how long it takes him to dress.

But soon they are distracted by the appearance of the woman who arrives with him. She carries a parasol, which quickly blows inside out with the first gust of Bering Sea wind. More remarkable, her considerable hair is piled on the top of her head, with feathers and ornaments protruding from the top of it. Her long dress creates an even greater sensation. Not only is it extraordinarily and impractically long, dragging in the mud behind her, but there is something very obviously wrong with this woman's rear end. It sticks way out! Her fashionable bustle inspires hours of speculation. Can that really be her rear end? Or is there some sort of artificial padding back there? No one dares ask or check.

A few days later, Mrs. Fatfanny exits her cabin and begins making a lot of clanging noise in front of the skuuluuq. The Real People are startled by this, peeking out their doors and windows to see what is causing the commotion. When they see the pale and sickly lady with her odd hairdo and weirder posterior violently ringing her bell, they think it odd but react with no particular alarm or concern. Everyone pretty much goes back to bed, leaving the teachers perplexed and perturbed that no scholars have rushed forth, pencil boxes in hand, eager to begin the school year.

In fact, no one shows up for school that week. No one realizes they are supposed to. Only gradually do the teachers become more aggressive recruiters, setting out each morning to pounce on unsuspecting pupils. One teacher fetches a child as the other guards the door to prevent escape, then they continue the hunt. Eventually they manage to fill the benches and get all their students positioned behind their desks.

Now, in perfectly clear and precise English, they begin to explain, using charades, that they expect the children to scamper quickly to the school once the bell rings.

"When we ring the bell," gestures Mrs. Fatfanny, "you hurry here to the school."

The pupils nod their agreement. But the situation remains confusing. In August, the bell is rung shortly after dawn. In October, it starts ringing a little before dawn. In December, they're ringing it in the middle of the night! No one can predict when they will ring the silly thing, and the kids are always in trouble—"late for school." It is safer not to attend at all; the dropout rate is very high.

We know that although most village schools offered only eight years of schooling, there were no graduation ceremonies for the first two or three decades. Continuing to live their traditional subsistence lifestyle, parents, kids and extended families ventured off into the wilderness in search of food—continuing to hunt, fish and gather as they had for thousands of years, leaving the frustrated and often furious missionary teachers home alone for weeks on end. There was really no choice. Everyone was needed to perform their traditional chores to sustain the Human Beings. Keeping these odd strangers happy was of relative, but hardly paramount, importance.

Dedicated assimilationists, the teachers believed their mission was to avoid, as Dr. Jackson often said, *Indian wars and reservations*. Alaska would escape the evils of the first two chapters in the national story of race relations. There would be no extermination or removal of Native Peoples here. Eskimos and Indians in the Alaska Territory would be painlessly assimilated into the American "melting pot," as laborers, to be employed by white settlers in mining, farming and transportation. To advance the assimilationist agenda, no instruction could be offered in the local languages. In fact, all use of indigenous tribal languages was forbidden at school.

"And another thing," the teacher would exclaim, "you must not speak your language on school property during school hours!" There was no charade adequate to convey School Rule Number Two and few students grasped it. Consequently, when a younger pupil opened his mouth and only Inupiaq came out, that child was immediately and violently disciplined, with a slap across the face or some iodine on the tongue. The entire student body learned quickly not to speak at all, and the school became a very silent place for the first twenty years of its existence.

Only gradually, after decades, did a few begin to succeed at their studies. After about thirty years, eighth grade graduation ceremonies became regular features of village springtime celebrations. Then the teachers focused their efforts on recruiting the most promising teens to enroll in something called "high school." No one in the traditional villages had actually seen a "high school"—these were some place far away. For over seventy years, Alaska had no Native secondary schools. Going to "high school" meant leaving the Territory.

This was not a uniquely Alaskan situation. Native American students from the West were normally deported eastward to attend high school at institutions like the Carlisle Indian School, outside Harrisburg, Pennsylvania. The hope was that having succeeded, graduates would not want to return to their distant home and family but would seek employment, and like the children of immigrants from Europe, "melt" into the general population.

But at least three factors precluded this. First, Native Americans were racially distinct, and racism against them made assimilation virtually impossible. Second, Natives—unlike their immigrant counterparts—had not willingly left their homeland in order to assume a new identity. They had been forcibly moved across the continent, and remained eager to return home and resume their lives and identity as Native Americans. Third, assimilation was not attractive to the majority of Indian and Eskimo people because of their affinity for their homelands. To "melt" into the dominant society (even if they could), was to conspire in the demise and extinction of one's own language and culture.

No Native American could assimilate without bearing a tremendous burden of guilt and grief for the trade-offs they were forced to make. If the first generation experienced frustration and confusion as they ended their schooling, the next generation, even as they earned their high school diplomas, became increasingly angry and bitter, as well as guilt-ridden and depressed. By the time the third generation started school the community was suffering tremendous self-doubt. They could see the benefits of assimilation but could not embrace this as a long-term solution. In their world, assimilation means the rejection of one's world view, the conscious decision to play someone else's game of life, to abandon one's story in order to pretend to have been born into another. Assimilation in this sense requires one to live falsely, to deny one's own heritage and identity and to masquerade forever as something one is not.

For the Native American, to assimilate carries a social, economic and political penalty as well. The dominant society looks upon those who cannot or will not assimilate as backward, stupid, incompetent or ungrateful. When Native people affirm their ancient culture, they are seen as dropouts from modernity. To the extent that they capitulate to the conformist pressure, they are viewed as having betrayed their own culture and people. Assimilation presents every Native American with an unsolvable dilemma.

Looking around after seventy years of assimilationist education, Natives began to doubt their own competence. Without expressing this attitude too explicitly or openly, they began to think that there was something wrong with them. White folks, they recognized, seemed to have no problem succeeding in school. They seemed to be born with a birth certificate in one hand and high school diploma or even a college degree in the other. Natives, on the other hand, performed poorly. "We always get to be second, never first," one young woman told me. "Always a Tonto, the loyal assistant to the main guy, never a Lone Ranger. We get to be teacher aides, not teachers, health aides, not doctors or nurses, legal aides, not lawyers. We just don't measure up. I guess we just can't."

Those two words, *we can't*, contain a deadly falsehood. *We can't* is the sound of the victims blaming themselves. Other folks *can* but *we can't*—an ironic admission of failure for Native people who have creatively survived in some of the planet's most threatening and dangerous environments.

As drugs and alcohol were introduced to the population, the villages of Alaska erupted in an epidemic of anti-social and self-destructive behavior. Visiting the northwestern part of the state one springtime, I discovered that every local high school's yearbook was dedicated to a member of the senior class who had died prior to graduation. In some communities there were two such students; in one there were four. All had taken their own lives. And there had been several unsuccessful suicide attempts among the surviving classmates. Even more had died in preventable accidents, having taken unnecessary risks in an already dangerous country. Others had expressed their pent up anger and bitterness in socially inappropriate and destructive ways, lashing out, almost always under the influence of illicit drugs or bootlegged alcohol, committing violent crimes against their own family and friends.

After more than a hundred years of assimilationism, the contemporary Native population continues to suffer from violence dealt to others and to themselves. At this stage, the government intervenes with "help." For suicides we need a hotline. For drugs we need counseling. For bootleggers, we need more police. To stem the tide of anti-social behavior, we need stricter enforcement, bigger jails, tougher sentencing. The government appropriates millions of dollars. Social workers, medical care providers, counselors, all sorts of preventative programs and interventions have flooded into the region. As these new "outside" professionals establish their presence, they offer their expertise to the locals. But the more external, non-reciprocal help that is imported, the more dependent, depressed, confused and frustrated the population becomes. The more others try to help, the worse the problems get.

It has taken more than a hundred years to put this cycle of dependence, confusion, frustration, anxiety, anger, bitterness, guilt and grief into operation. It has produced an overwhelming sense of nihilism ("nothing matters, I don't matter, you don't matter, no one matters") that provides the context for the widespread use of drugs and alcohol.

A population suffering depression, as the dominant culture did during the Great Depression, will resort to pain-numbing anesthesia, the cheapest form of which is alcohol. No one can understand drinking as a problem without first understanding alcohol as a solution. This "solution" may have a very short effect and may even produce a new level of problems, but people get drunk to forget, to have some relief from the pain and strain of being alive. And then, under the influence, all the anger and pain and guilt and sadness they keep carefully concealed when sober, erupts in a torrent that often harms, destroys, kills.

The way out of this tragic cycle lies within the Real People themselves. No temporary hired professional can really change the dynamics of the dependence cycle. No one from outside the community can transform it, make it a better, happier, healthier place. The United Nations cannot pass a unanimous resolution declaring that a particular Alaskan Native village will be much improved in two or three years. The U.S. Congress, the state legislature, these institutions lack the power to transform a town or a neighborhood. Only its residents and citizens can change the situation, and no one else. "We can't" is a lie that is literally killing Native people today.

A reawakening, a revitalization of the traditional culture, the Way of the Human Being, lies at the foundation of a new chapter that is beginning to emerge in many regions. Young people are reaffirming their belief in themselves, in their communities, in their people, and rejecting the false dichotomies that have created the old either/or dilemma. They are embracing both identities and claim both as legitimately their own. We can be who we are, and we can live successfully in the modern world. We can do both. We *must* do both. That is how we become Real People. We adapt. We change, but we also hold on to all that is good, true and beautiful in our story, in our way of life, in our culture.

That is not only a challenge and task for Alaska Natives, but the essential need of every Human Being on the planet today. As Alaska Natives have always known, after the long, cold, dark night, if the Human Beings do what they should and must do, there comes, inevitably, a new dawn and a never-ending day.

Inupiat drummers. *Photo by Bill Hess*

Young Tlingit Dancers at the First Annual Conference of Tlingit Clans and Tribes, Haines-Klukwan, May 1993. *Photo by Peter Metcalfe*

Preceding page: Blanket toss preview. *Photo by Bill Hess*

Top: The late Eileen McClean campaigning for the legislature. *Photo by Bill Hess*

Bottom: Orthodox church service. *Photo by Bill Hess*

BIBLIOGRAPHY AND SUGGESTED ADDITIONAL READINGS

ALASKAN CULTURES

Alaska Native Ways, introduction by Will Mayo, Graphic Arts Center Publishing, Portland, OR (2002)

Crossroads of Continents, by William Fitzhugh and Aron Crowell, Smithsonian Institution, Washington, DC (1988)

Native Peoples of Alaska, by Steve Langdon, Greatland Graphics, Anchorage, AK (1993)

Russian America: the Forgotten Frontier, by Barbara Smith and Redmond Barnett, Washington State Historical Society, Tacoma, WA (1990)

Alaska Native Languages, Past, Present and Future, by Michael Krauss, University of Alaska, Fairbanks, AK (1980)

Village Journey, by Thomas Berger, Hill & Wang, New York, NY (1985)

TRADITIONAL CULTURES

In the Absence of the Sacred, by Jerry Mander, Sierra Club Books, San Francisco, CA (1991)

The Sacred and the Profane, by Mircea Eliade, Harcourt, Inc., New York, NY (1987)

Through Indian Eyes, Reader's Digest Association, Pleasantville, NY (1995)

Rites and Symbols of Initiation, by Mircea Eliade, Harper and Row, New York, NY (1958)

Shamanism, by Mircea Eliade, Princeton University Press, Princeton, NJ (1964)

The Island Within, by Richard Nelson, University of Washington, Seattle, WA (1989)

STORYTELLING

Life Lived as a Story, by Julie Cruikshank, University of Nebraska Press, (1990)

Native American Oral Traditions, by Larry Evers and Barre Toelken, Utah State University, Logan, UT, (1990)

ALUTIIQ CULTURE

Looking Both Ways, edited by Aron Crowell, Amy Steffian and Gordon Pullar, UAF Press, Fairbanks, AK (2001)

Birth and Rebirth on an Alaskan Island, by Joanne B. Mulcahy, University of Georgia Press, Athens, GA (2001)

Time to Dance, by Michael Rostad, A.T. Publishing, Anchorage, AK (1988)

UNANGAN HISTORY

Orthodox Alaska, by Michael Oleksa, SVS Press, Crestwood, NY (1992)

The Etholen Collection, National Museum, Helsinki, Finland (1990)

Conflicting Visions in Alaskan Education, by Richard Dauenhauer, Alaska Native Language Center, University of Alaska, Fairbanks, AK (1998)

A Century of Servitude, by Dorothy Knee Jones, University Press of America, Lanham, MD (1980)

When the Wind was a River, by Dean Kohlhoff, University of Washington Press, Seattle, WA (1995)

Moments Rightly Placed, by Ray Hudson, Epicenter Press, Portland, OR (1999)

Seven Words for Wind, by Summer MacLeish, Epicenter Press, Portland, OR (1998)

YUP'IK CULTURE

INUA, William Fitzhugh and Susan Kaplan, Smithsonian Institute, Washington, DC (1982)

Always Getting Ready, James Baker, University of Washington Press, Seattle, WA (1993)

The Living Tradition of Yup'ik Masks, Ann Fieniup-Riordan, University of Washington Press, Seattle, WA (1996)

Yuuyararq, The Way of the Human Being, Harold Napoleon, Alaska Northwest Publishing (2001)

YUP'IK STORIES

Yup'ik Lore (1981) and *One Must Arrive with a Story to Tell*, Lower Kuskokwim School District, Bethel, AK (1995)

Paul John's Stories for Future Generations (Qulirat Qanemcitllu) translated by Sophie Shield, University of Washington Press, Seattle, WA (2003)

YUP'IK HISTORY

Journals of Iakov Netsvetov, translated by Lydia Black, Limestone Press, Kingston, ON, (1984)

The Yup'ik Eskimo, edited by Ann Finiup-Riordan, Limestone Press, Kingston, ON (1988) and *The Real People and the Children of Thunder* (1991)

Russia in North America, Proceedings of the Second International Conference, edited by Richard Pierce, Limestone Press (1987)

Must One Way of Life Die for Another to Live? edited by Art Davidson, Yubiktak Bista, Bethel, AK (1974)

Harmonius to Dwell, by James Henkleman and Kurt Vitt, Moravian Seminary, Bethel, AK (1985)

For additional resources readers are advised to access the Alaska Native Knowledge Network web page at <ankn.uaf.edu/aeb.html>

TRADITIONAL VALUES OF ALASKA

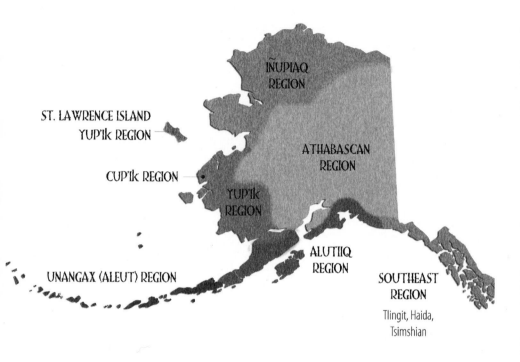

INUPIAQ REGION

ST. LAWRENCE ISLAND YUP'Ik REGION

CUP'Ik REGION

YUP'Ik REGION

ATHABASCAN REGION

UNANGAX (ALEUT) REGION

ALUTIIQ REGION

SOUTHEAST REGION
Tlingit, Haida, Tsimshian

BRISTOL BAY YUP'IK VALUES

- Have respect for our land and its resources at all times
- Be helpful to one another
- Share with others whenever possible
- Respect and care for other's property
- Respect spiritual values
- Learn hunting and outdoor survival skills
- Provide for and take good care of your family
- Through love, respect your children
- Respect your elders
- Work hard and don't be lazy
- Refrain from alcohol and drug use
- Learn, preserve, and be proud of the Native way of life

Approved by Esther Ilutsik, Ciulistet Research Association

CUP'IK VALUES

- Help other people
- Help with family chores and needs
- Early to bed and early to rise
- Provide time to see how your life is going
- There's always time to play AFTER your work is done
- Pingnatugyaraq: learn to do things yourself
- Respect and honor your elders
- Always show good behavior
- Listen to all advice given to you
- Remember what you are taught and told
- Respect other people's belongings
- Respect the animals you catch for food
- Gather knowledge and wisdom from the elders
- Never give up in trying to do what you set your mind on

  Authorized by John Pingayaq, Cultural Heritage Program Director/Teacher, Kashunamiut School District, Chevak

SAINT LAWRENCE ISLAND YUP'IK VALUES

- Listen with your heart and mind
- Honor Family
- Give Service to others
- Never give up
- Respect all living things
- Remember advice of elders
- Plan for the future
- Be independent
- Avoid laziness
- Gather knowledge and wisdom

  Approved by Anders Apassingok Sr., Gambell Elder

UNANGAX̂ (ALEUT) VALUES

- Udigdada. E / Udigida. W / Share.
- Tutada. E & W / Listen.
- Txin anguyni{ta}ulux. E / Txin manitalagada. W / Don't be boastful.
- Agitaasitxin i{amnaasada. E / An}a}inas i}amanaasada. W / Be kind to other people.
- Agitaasiin sismida. E / An}a}inas kiduda. W / Help others.
- Tuman tana{ agliisaa{tan. E / Tana{ agliisada. W / Take care of the land.
- Tuman ala}u{ agliisaa{tan. E / Ala}u{ agliisada. W / Take care of the sea/ocean.
- Tuman taanga{ agliisaa{txin. E / Taanga{ haqayaasada. W / Take care of the water.
- Manachin ilam axtalakan agliisaachin. E / Ana}is mal agumis ilam axtalagada. W / Do not do anything to excess.
- Txin ugutada. E / Qa}atada. W / Be happy.
- I}ayuu{txin, ana}im atxa}ingin agachan madada. E / Txin sakaa}atal ana}is mada. W / Behave yourself: Do the things you know are right.
- Chxadalagaa{txin. E / Chxalagada. W / Don't steal.
- Adluuda}i}ulux E / Adalulagada. W / Don't lie.
- Ludakiim axtax samtaaxtxin. E / Ludaa}is, tukus ama uchiitilas sahnga{tada. W Respect Elders (including parents, teachers, & community members).
- Agitaasiin samtasaa{txin. E / Agitaadaan sahnga{tada. W / Respect your peers.
- Kayutuu{txin. E / Kayutuda. W / Be strong.
- Agitaasiin matanangin imin gidu}iisalagaa{txin. E / Silaa txin gikuun alagada. W / Don't be envious of what belongs to another.
- An}a}i{ i{amana{ i{talix kayux i{amana{ atxa{talix manaa imin ugutaasalix aa{txin. E / An}a}ina{ i}amanas manaa ngaan hi{tada. W / Admire one who does well by honest means.
- Maamin i{tanatxin madada. E / Ana}is maamis hi{taqaan aguun mada. W / Don't make promises quickly, but keep those you make.
- An}a}iisanatxin an}a}im agitaasingin agachan liidalix an}a}iisada. E / Matal an}a}iikaan agacha an}a}isada. W / Live like you want people to see you live.
- Igilnaa{na{txin. E / Qaqatulagada. W / Don't be greedy.
- Sla{, a}ada{, tugida{, kayux sdan tunum manginulux kugan i}ad}ulux. E / Sla{, a}adgi{, ama sdas hadangiin i}amana{ agacha tunu{taasada. W / Don't talk bad about the weather or the sun, the moon, or the stars.
- Agitaasaan adaan tunum i{amnanginulux i}ad}ulux. E / An}a}ina{ adalus hadaan hil}ada}ulax. W / Don't slander another person.

- Kadaan axtaa}ana{txin. E / Kadamis agalagada. W / Don't get ahead of yourself.
- Adu{tanaan akidada. E / Adut akida. W / Pay your debts.
- Qaqamii}u{. E / Qaqamii}u{. W / Subsistence.
- Tunuun ugunu{talakan an}a}ii{txin. E / Unangam Tunuu ugunu{talagada. W / Don't forget your Unangan Language.

VALUES OF THE UNANGAN/UNANGAS

- An}a}iisi{ matanaan imin i{amnaku{. Ana}i{ ukunachin imchin ugutaasaamchim a}na{txichin. /An}a}iisiin siga{ imis aku{ mal sigaan inixsiisada.
  Life is gifted to you. What you make of it is your gift in return.
- Tuman ilaanu}itxin, Unangan maqa{tadqangin mataa}in matakun. / An}a}iisiin, ilaazat ama Ulamis an}a}inangis maqa{singis ida{talagada.
  Know your family tree, relations and people's history.
- Tana}nangin I}ayuusalix an}a}iimchin a}na{txichin. / Tana{, Ala}u{ ama slum imuunuu huzuu ana}im ana}in}is sahnga{tada.
  Live with and respect the land, sea, and all nature.
- Wan ala}um ilan ana}im an}a}inangin usuu Aguu}u{ agach ngiin a}iqaa. / Algas ama ana}im an}a}ingis huzungis Aguu}um agacha ngiin a}iqaa haqataasada.
  Respect and be aware of the creator in all living things.
- Txin achigalix an}a}igumin anuxtanatxin a{saasaduuku{txin. / Huzugaan txin achiga{ agacha mada ama txin sakaa}atada.
  Always learn and maintain a balance.
- Qaqamii}u{ qalgadam ukulganaa ngiin ugutaasakun. / Qaqamii}u{ qalgada{An}a}i{ ngiin a{tanaa aku{.
  Subsistence is sustenance for the life.
- Unangam tunuu unangqasining asix tunu{talaa}naqing. Unangan anaan Uku{tach{iku{. / Unangam tunuu Unangas alganaa ukuchxiza{ ama huzu{ ngiin tunu{tach{iza{.
  Our language defines who we are and lets us communicate with one another.
  Authorized by Moses Dirks, President, Association of Unangan/s Educators and the Elders Academy

KODIAK ALUTIIQ CULTURAL VALUES

- Our Elders
- Our heritage language
- Family and the kinship of our ancestors and living relatives
- Ties to our homeland
- A subsistence lifestyle, respectful of and sustained by the natural world
- Traditional arts, skills and ingenuity
- Faith and a spiritual life, from ancestral beliefs to the diverse faiths of today
- Sharing: we welcome everyone
- Sense of humor
- Learning by doing, observing and listening
- Stewardship of the animals, land, sky and waters
- Trust
- Our people: we are responsible for each other and ourselves
- Respect for self, others and our environment is inherent in all of these values.

  Authorized by Teri Schneider, Coordinator for Native Educators of the Alutiiq Region, Kodiak

SOUTHEAST TRADITIONAL TRIBAL VALUES

- Discipline and Obedience to the Traditions of our Ancestors
- Respect for Self, Elders and Others
- Respect for Nature and Property
- Patience
- Pride in Family, Clan and Traditions is found in Love, Loyalty and Generosity
- Be Strong in Mind, Body and Spirit
- Humor
- Hold Each Other Up
- Listen Well and with Respect
- Speak with Care
- We are Stewards of the Air, Land and Sea
- Reverence for Our Creator
- Live in Peace and Harmony
- Be Strong and Have Courage

  Authorized by Edward K. Thomas, President of the Central Council Tlingit and Haida Indian Tribes of Alaska

NORTH SLOPE INUPIAQ VALUES

- Sharing - Aviktuaqatigiigñiq
- Compassion – Nagliktuutiqaåniq
- Family and Kinship – Iḷagiigñiq
- Avoidance of Conflict – Paaqæaktautaiññiq
- Hunting Traditions – Aÿuniallaniq
- Humor – Quvianåuniq
- Love and Respect for Our Elders and One Another – Piqpakkutuqaåniq suli Qiksiksrautiqaåniq Utuqqanaanun Allanullu
- Respect for Nature – Qiksriksrautiqaåniq Iñuuniaåvigmun
- Spiritually – Ukpiqqutiqaåniq
- Cooperation – Paammaaåiigñiq
- Knowledge of Language - Iñupiuraallaniq
- Humility - Qiñuiññiq

  Authorized by Fannie Kuutuuq Akpik, Inupiaq Studies, Iḷisaåvik College

NORTHWEST ARCTIC INUPIAQ VALUES

- Knowledge of Language
- Knowledge of Family Tree
- Sharing
- Humility
- Respect for Others
- Love for Children
- Cooperation
- Hard Work
- Respect for Elders
- Respect for Nature
- Avoid Conflict
- Family Roles
- Humor
- Spirituality
- Domestic Skills
- Hunter Success
- Responsibility to Tribe

  Authorized by Siikauraq Martha Whiting, Assistant to the Mayor, Northwest Arctic Borough

ATHABASCAN VALUES

- Self sufficiency
- Hard Work
- Care and provision for the family
- Family relations
- Unity
- Honor
- Honesty
- Fairness
- Love for Children
- Sharing
- Caring
- Village Cooperation
- Responsibility to Village
- Respect for Elders and Others
- Respect for Knowledge
- Wisdom from Life Experiences
- Respect for the Land
- Respect for Nature
- Practice of Traditions
- Honoring Ancestors
- Spirituality

Authorized by Cathi Ipalook, Cultural Programs Director, Denakkanaaga

FATHER MICHAEL OLEKSA

Father Michael Oleksa, PhD, was born in Allentown, Pennsylvania. He came to Alaska in 1970 from St. Vladimir's Seminary in New York at the invitation of the Alutiiq village of Old Harbor on Kodiak Island. Over the next three decades he served as a Russian Orthodox priest in over a dozen Alaska Native villages. In 1988 he completed his doctoral degree at the Orthodox Theological Faculty in Presov, Slovakia, with an emphasis in Native Alaskan History during the Alaska Russian period (1741-1867).

Recognized as an "Elder" by the Alaska Federation of Natives, a Distinguished Public Servant by the Board of Regents of the University of Alaska, and honored by the Alaska State Legislature and the National Governors Association, Dr. Oleksa is a storyteller who seeks to foster greater understanding across boundaries of race and culture—as he has said, "to make The Great Land even greater."

Father Oleksa currently lives in Anchorage with his Yup'ik wife, Xenia, where he serves as parish priest for St. Alexis Orthodox Church and teaches at Alaska Pacific University.